The Covid Conspiracy

The Cure for Covid and the Plot to Hide it from the World

Mark W. Swarbrick

Copyright © 2021 by Mark Swarbrick

Previous publications by Mark Swarbrick...

Theistic Evolution: Did God Create Through Evolution?

Heavenly Miracles: True Stories of Supernatural Intervention

To Mormons with Love: A Pilgrimage Through Mormon History and Doctrine

King James Onlyism: Is the KJV the Best Bible Version?

End of Days: What the Bible Says Happens Next

Catholicism: The Hidden Truth About Catholicism

Life After Death: What Happens When We Die?

Swaggartism: The Strange Doctrines of Jimmy Swaggart Ministries

Hidden History: The Untold Story of the Democratic Party

Truly Amazing (Book I) The Real Story of Adam and Eve

These titles may be purchased at:

https://www.Amazon.com/author/markswarbrick

Legal Disclaimer
Read This First!

The author is not a doctor or licensed healthcare practitioner or provider and does not claim to have any formal medical background. This book contains the author's political, religious, and other opinions protected by the First Amendment of the U.S. Constitution, which guarantees that the right of free speech and freedom of the press shall not be infringed. The author makes no claim to be able to cure any cause, condition, or disease. The information contained herein is merely the opinion of a layman individual and should not be construed to be medical advice. This writing is for entertainment purposes only. The research and information covered in this book is open to the public domain for discussion and in no way breaches or breaks the boundaries of the law in any state of the United States of America where the author resides.

The author is not liable, either expressly or in an implied manner, nor claims any responsibility for any emotional or physical problems that may occur directly or indirectly from reading this book. This book details the author's personal experiences with, and opinions about, current medical concerns that are the topic of much public discussion and debate. The author and publisher are providing this book and its contents on an "as is" basis and make no representations or warranties of any kind with respect to this book or its contents. The author and publisher disclaim all such representations and warranties, including for example warranties of merchantability and healthcare for a particular purpose. In addition, the author and publisher do not represent or warrant that the information accessible via this book is accurate, complete, or current.

Any statements made about products or services that may or may not be mentioned have not been evaluated by the U.S. Food and Drug Administration. The information contained herein is not intended to diagnose, treat, cure, or prevent any condition or disease. Please consult with your own physician or healthcare specialist regarding what may appear to be suggestions or recommendations made in this book. Except as specifically stated in this book, neither the author or publisher, nor any authors, contributors, or other representatives will be liable for damages arising out of or in connection with the use of this book. This is a comprehensive limitation of liability that applies to all damages of any kind, including (without limitation) compensatory; direct, indirect, or consequential damages; loss of data, income, or profit; loss of or damage to property and claims of third parties.

Printed in the United States of America.
1st Edition

Table of Contents

1

The Cure for Covid

There is a cure for Covid-19. Yes, you heard me right – a cure for Covid. Now hold on – before the thought police come knocking on my door, let me clarify. To be technically correct, I should say there is an effective therapeutic medicine available that is of proven benefit to Covid sufferers. That is how the medical establishment would like it to be phrased. Doctors don't like to speak of cures. They speak of therapies or remission, but not cures.

I am not a doctor. I am just a country boy from the Midwest with some basic horse sense, so I don't phrase things in such a nuanced manner. To my way of thinking, when you have a deadly disease that may kill you, and you take a medicine that results in the disease vanishing, that is a cure, at least that's what I call it. That's just my personal opinion. The fact remains, there is a medication so safe and effective that many people with Covid who have used it call it a cure.

While I am on the subject of "I am not a doctor," let me elaborate a bit more so that I don't get sued by anyone or harassed by the FDA. I alluded to this in my disclaimer but I want to include this in the text of the book itself. If you have not read the disclaimer, go read it now. I will say this one more time before we proceed: Talk with a licensed medical doctor before you take any medicines mentioned in this book. Don't take medicines without a legal prescription. Follow the advice of your doctor and if you don't like what your doctor says and does, find another licensed doctor.

What I am going to tell you should not be considered medical advice, but merely constitutes my personal opinions that are protected under the free-speech and freedom-of-the-press clauses of the 1st Amendment to the Constitution of the United States. Any threats of legal action from entities of Big Pharma intended to intimidate me into silence will be considered by myself as an attempt done in collusion with the government to deprive me of the aforementioned constitutional rights and such threats will be forthwith forwarded to my attorney for legal action. Furthermore, none of the products mentioned in this book are sold by me. I have no connection with them whatsoever and receive no monetary reward from their sale. Therefore, the Federal Trade Commission has no jurisdiction and cannot legally inhibit the free expression of my personal opinions.

Now, where was I? Oh yes, the cure for Covid – excuse me – I mean to say, the therapeutic medicine of noteworthy efficacy that many doctors around the world are prescribing to Covid patients. I am not talking about vaccines or the expensive new experimental drugs that Big Pharma is pushing, such as remdesivir or molnupiravir. I am talking about an old drug that has been around for decades, is very cheap, is fully FDA approved for human use, has been taken by billions of people around the world, and is safer than aspirin or acetaminophen.

Some powerful people don't want you to know about this remedy. They don't want you to get it or use it, even though many doctors say that it can save your life. Some people are desperate to cover up the truth about it, so much so that they have launched a powerful disinformation and intimidation campaign to discourage and prevent people from getting this medication.

The story I am about to tell you is not some tinfoil-hat kooky conspiracy from the dark side of the Internet. What I am going to explain is documented truth that has been attested to by numerous doctors and researchers as well as people who worked on President Trump's Covid task force that was organized to get effective therapeutics to the American people as fast as possible. The obstruction, lies, and obfuscations that the deep state and Big Pharma launched against this effort have led to countless Covid deaths.

Despite the wicked efforts of certain powerful people, it is still possible to get this medicine. I will explain how to get it legally and at a reasonable price. Every household in America should have this medicine in their cupboard. You should have it on hand in case you or a loved one comes down with Covid. It takes a little time to get the prescription and have it filled, so you can't wait until you get sick to figure out how to buy it. You need the medicine on hand so you can take it immediately if you test positive for Covid.

I would not expect that you would run out and buy some of this medicine just because I say you should. You need to know the facts for yourself and you need to hear the truth from medical doctors. Then you need to know how to find a doctor that will prescribe it for you. I will tell you where to find the information you need. But first, let me tell you the story of the cure for Covid, how it was discovered, who is using it, who wants to bury that story, and why.

Count on Yourself – Not the Government

Covid-19 is nothing to take lightly. It can kill and you don't know who it is going to get next. For some people, it is an inconvenient cold. For others, it is a battle of life and death. It can destroy your lungs and leave you drowning and gasping for each breath. I have had several friends and family get Covid. Some of them have made the exact same

8

statement to me: *"It is the sickest I have ever been in my life!"*

You can't count on a vaccine to protect you one-hundred percent. The government's position has been that if you're vaccinated you are perfectly safe. The recent Covid death of General Powell, who was vaccinated, disproves that. One of my doctors recently made this statement to me: *"Any healthcare worker will tell you that we are seeing just as many vaccinated people with Covid as unvaccinated."* I am not against vaccines. They can make the symptoms less severe. I have been vaccinated myself, as I am elderly with comorbidities that make me high risk. More on that terrible experience later. I'm just telling you what all the doctors are now saying; the vaccines are not as effective as had been expected. Some vaccinated people are still dying from Covid. And according to the CDC, many thousands have died from the vaccine.

The decision of vaccination should be a matter of discussion between a person and their doctor. It is not something that politicians should decide for you and it should never be forced on anyone. Let the politicians stick to politics and let the medical professionals practice medicine. That is my opinion, for what it is worth to you.

It is up to people to make their own decisions about their health. Sadly, we live in a time when you cannot believe everything the government says. You might not be able to count on your doctor giving you what you need if you come down with Covid. It depends on your doctor. He might do the right thing and he might not. In an ideal world, your doctor would decide himself what is best for you. Unfortunately, that is not exactly how it works. Your doctor's hands may be tied by the clinic he or she works for. Doctors take a risk if they prescribe medicines outside the parameters set by the government bureaucracy composed of the FDA, AMA, CDC, NIH, and the WHO.[1]

I asked my doctor a year ago what he would do for me if I got Covid. At the time, the best medication for Covid according to my research was the anti-malaria drug hydroxychloroquine (HCQ). I told him I would want an off-label prescription of this if I came down with Covid. He told me that not only would he not prescribe it, but that if I were to get Covid, he would send me home with no treatment, and when I got so sick that I couldn't breathe, and felt like I was dying, then I could go to the Emergency Room. What a horrible way to practice medicine! Why are they doing this?

Here is why. Most doctors will only give you medicine that is recommended for a specific ailment as determined by these authorities, and as we shall see, the judgment of said authorities has been compromised by greed and corruption. Most medical doctors are good soldiers that toe the party line when it comes to only prescribing what is approved by the powers that be. They can find themselves in trouble if they don't. Prescribing a medicine "off-label" for a condition that the medicine was not originally intended, may lead to legal problems for a doctor or a clinic, particularly if something goes wrong. Nevertheless, many medicines are prescribed off-label. It is actually a fairly common practice. But for reasons we shall discuss, prescribing off-label for Covid has become a political hot-potato.

With Covid-19, many doctors have stated that early treatment is essential. The drugs I am going to tell you about are most effective if taken in the early stages of the disease. These medicines are not available from your local Walgreens or CVS anymore, so if you wait until you are

---

[1] FDA=Food and Drug Administration, AMA=American Medical Association, CDC=Center for Disease Control, NIH, National Institutes of Health, WHO=World Health Organization

sick before trying to get medicine, you are going to be in the second stage of the disease before you ever get the medication.

Powerful entities are preventing people from getting the cure from their local doctor and pharmacy. Even if your local doctor wrote you a prescription for it, Walgreens and CVS will not fill it. They have filled prescriptions for this medicine for years, but that has all changed in the past year. It would seem they have already received their marching orders. What orders and from whom? Read on.

2

Who, What and Why?

In Chapter 7 we will delve into what this medicine is. I am eager to get to that. But once you see the proof of the safety and efficacy of the medication you are going to have some serious questions. Who are these unscrupulous persons that are keeping life-saving medicine from those who need it? Why are they letting people die needlessly? Let's go into all that first.

There are actually three groups involved and they all have their own reasons, but they have all conspired together to suppress the truth. At the heart of the conspiracy is Big Pharma. By that, I mean primarily the pharmaceutical companies that discover and produce our medicines and the agencies that approve them. Complicit in the deception are the mass media news agencies, the socialist deep state, the current Biden administration, and last, but certainly not least, Dr. Anthony Fauci, who is probably the most culpable. More about him later.

The FDA, CDC, WHO, and the NIH are all part of Big Pharma, as the CEOs and top officials of those organizations are basically one and the same as those who run the drug companies. For example, FDA officials frequently were previously employed by pharmaceutical companies and often go back to work for them after their stint with the FDA and vice versa.

There is a revolving door between these medical organizations and the drug companies and this is a huge conflict of interest.

This is not how it was supposed to be. The FDA is supposed to be an unbiased third party, a government entity that provides oversite over drug companies. In reality, it is not a disinterested party. It is the fox guarding the henhouse. The federal regulatory agencies have the interests of the drug companies at heart, and the main goal of the drug companies is large profits.

Why Are They Doing This?

That answers the question of who. Now for the why. Does the proverbial statement, "follow the money," give you a clue? After the man-made coronavirus escaped from the bio-weapons laboratory in Communist China and infected the world, pharmaceutical companies got busy trying to invent an expensive new medicine that would save the world and make them wealthier than their wildest dreams. If you own the patent on a medication that every person in the entire world needs, you will have achieved unprecedented wealth and power.

Once the vaccines were released, Big Pharma had their cash cow that brought in the trillions of dollars they coveted. But the drug companies want to keep this unprecedented amount of revenue coming in forever. For that, they need to vaccinate not just elderly people who need it, but every man, woman, and child in the world, and now they are telling us that regular booster shots will be necessary forever. That way the astronomical riches will flow into Big Pharma in perpetuity. Could it be that they want this so bad they will say or do anything to make it happen? The reader must decide. I realize this all sounds quite cynical. Please reserve judgment until you have seen the evidence.

Pfizer, one of the major vaccine manufacturers, is now encouraging five to eleven-year-old children to get vaccinated, even though it is common knowledge that children are not endangered by the virus, except in very rare circumstances. The immune function of children is so strong that the virus is quickly defeated. There is great concern among many people about adverse reactions to the vaccines, especially regarding giving them to children who don't need them. Doctors are on record as expressing their concern that the benefits do not outweigh the risks in the case of young children.

In response to this public concern, the drug companies have labeled concerned parents as criminals. For example, in push-back to this legitimate parental concern, the CEO of Pfizer, Albert Bourla, said that people who spread what he calls "misinformation" on Covid-19 vaccines are "criminals." Bourla said, *"These people are criminals...they're criminals because they have literally cost millions of lives."* In response to this, one news anchor of the mass media responded, *"And they should be treated as criminals."*

In other words, if people have concerns about the vaccines and report or discuss facts that disagree with the interests of Big Pharma, they should be "treated like criminals." How do we treat criminals? They are arrested, handcuffed, sent to prison, and sometimes executed. Apparently, the CEO of Pfizer and the news anchor are not aware that in America we have this thing called free speech. The 1st Amendment of the U.S. Constitution guarantees that you cannot be "treated like a criminal" for expressing your opinion.

So, pardon me Mr. Lord Pfizer King while I behave like a criminal and remind you that the CDC has reported 16,766 deaths[2] from the vaccines with 157,708 total

---

[2] *https://www.christianitydaily.com/articles/13646/20211018/senator-says-covid-vaccine-mandates-are-pointless-following-thousands-of-deaths-injuries-after-the-jabs.htm*

reported hospitalizations and 798,634 adverse reactions.[3] One young girl has been confined to a wheelchair with multiple neurological issues since being vaccinated. The horror stories abound. The fact is, in the opinion of many doctors, young healthy people don't need vaccines and for children especially, the benefit does not outweigh the inherent risk. I am sure that the lord of global elitists running Pfizer would like to lock me up as a criminal for having a discussion with people about this. He had better build a lot of very large prisons because half of America has the same concerns I do.

The vaccines are new mRNA – or Messenger RNA – vaccines. This type of vaccine has never received FDA approval in the past. They are still not fully FDA-approved but are released under an Emergency Use Authorization, which allows the circumvention of the normal long testing processes. Normal vaccines typically use a dead or inactive form of the virus. Not so with the new Covid vaccines. These use the new mRNA technology never before used on a massive scale.

A messenger RNA is a single-strand piece of instructions that tells a cell how to make something, such as a protein. A Covid vaccine contains mRNA that is coded to tell our body how to make a spike protein similar to the spike proteins that the virus has. Our cells then make this protein. The immune system sees the protein as something foreign and goes to work eliminating it, learning how in the process. If a person later gets infected with the coronavirus, the immune system can quickly and easily defeat it since it has already learned how to irradicate the spike protein.

We don't know what dangerous effects the new mRNA vaccines may have on people years down the road. For the elderly and infirm, the risk of the vaccine may be less than

---

[3] https://deathship.wordpress.com/2021/10/11/argentinian-doctor-shares-his-ivermectin-experience/

the risk of getting Covid. On the other hand, we don't know what long-term effects people may suffer later in life from contracting Covid. Chickenpox is an example of how viruses can have long-term effects. You may get Chickenpox as a youth, but 40 years later the dormant virus may resurface as Shingles. The truth is, we don't know the long-term effects, if any, of the virus or of the vaccines. How does one know what to do? Here is how: Study what doctors working with Covid patients say. Give that more credence than what politicians or government agencies tell you. Listen to the doctors, not the bureaucrats.

When I got my first Covid vaccine, I was told I would never get Covid. They lied. I have had Covid twice. When I got my second Covid vaccine, they told me it was safe. They lied again. The second shot made me deathly ill. I laid sick in bed for three weeks. Then my neck became paralyzed. It was terrifying. My wife drove me to the Emergency Room and after some injections and drugs, I eventually could move my neck again, though I still have stiffness and pain in my neck. I will never ever get another mRNA vaccination. The sickness, trouble, and pain it caused was worse than having Covid.

What is really unconscionable is that Big Pharma wants to criminalize any discussion of the matter and put people in jail for questioning their assertions. Reporting the truth is not misinformation and is not costing millions of lives, as they claim. But it may be costing Big Pharma billions of dollars, and that's where the real rub is. Why do they want to shut you up? Because they don't care about you, they care about profits. Where is the proof of this? It's coming. In the next chapter, we examine why Big Pharma has morphed into a political machine.

3

A Business or a Nation-State

It would be naïve to think of our large pharmaceutical companies as one would a typical American business. They are much more than that and just because they may be headquartered in the United States or were originally founded in the States, that does not mean we should think of them as a regular American company. They certainly don't view themselves that way.

These large multinational corporations have offices all over the world and sell to over a hundred different countries. Make no mistake – each of these drug companies is a nation-state in and of itself, whose prime concern is massive globalist dollars. What is best for average Americans living in rural America does not enter into their thinking. They have billions of dollars at their disposal and they have an interest in affecting elections and influencing governmental policy that will result in amassing more power and riches for themselves. That is who they are.

Peter Navarro knows this. He served in the Trump administration as the Assistant to the President, Director of Trade and Manufacturing Policy, and as the National Defense Production Act Policy Coordinator. He has dealt with numerous Big Pharma executives and he tells of the condescension that exudes from these international elitists.[4] As managers of their own global empire, they have their own foreign policy, domestic agenda, and worldview. Not

---

[4] *http://www.amzn.com/1737478501*

surprisingly, they view U.S. government executives as mere pawns in their powerful and manipulative hands.

Even the news organizations are under the thumb of Big Pharma. Fox News, a cable news outlet known for usually reporting the truth, is beholden to these powerful behemoths. Drug advertising is a huge revenue stream for Fox. If they were to report (pro or con) about any drug in a way that might negatively affect the balance sheet of their advertisers it could cost Fox significantly. Billions of dollars are at stake. Executives who call the shots at Fox News give strict orders to their newscasters, letting them know what is off-limits.

Big Pharma contributed massively to Biden's campaign and spent huge sums on anti-Trump commercials just before the election. Why would a drug company spend money to sway the vote? Let me explain. President Trump was outraged over Big Pharma's gouging of the American public on drug prices, selling cheaply to foreign countries but charging exorbitant prices for the same drug to Americans. He was fed up with Big Pharma's use of cheap sweatshop/slave labor in foreign countries.[5] He not only wanted fair prices for Americans but he pushed aggressively to bring pharmaceutical manufacturing and supply chains back to the States to provide American jobs.

President Trump issued executive orders to bring this about. One can imagine how the elite globalists reacted to interference by someone they looked down upon as nothing but a meddlesome politician – the President of the United States of America. If Big Pharma only disliked Trump before, now they saw him as the nemesis of their shareholders' interests.

---

[5] *https://www.clearharmony.net/articles/a40367-Slave-Labor-The-Secret-Weapon-the-Chinese-Communist-Party-Uses-to-Dominate-World-Trade.html*

Big Pharma was in the late stages of Trump Derangement Syndrome when they decreed that "Orange Man Bad" had to be stopped. And Big Pharma had the power and influence to do just that. With their massive financial resources, they controlled, to some extent, even the conservative press, not to mention their ability to support the reelection of candidates who did their bidding. And of course, the liberal press and the Democratic Party were already on their side. Big Pharma could count on their brother, Big Tech to help as well. Social media would take care of censoring any citizens from posting evidence of their nefarious plot. When you have nearly unlimited funding you can get a lot of people on your side. Who could stand against a conspiracy between the media, politicians, Big Tech, and Big Pharma? Apparently not even the president of the United States – he is history, for now anyway.

Step one was to make sure that vaccinations against Covid did not come out before the election. According to Presidential Assistant Peter Navarro, the Pfizer corporation deliberately delayed the release of their vaccine until after the 2020 election in order to hurt Trump's chance of re-election. Not one to make empty accusations, Navarro backs up his accusation with evidence. His book *In Trump Time*[6] effectively lays out the case that Pfizer intentionally delayed their vaccine by secretly pausing testing, which resulted in at least 50,000 unnecessary deaths. Are there really people so evil that they would let tens of thousands of people die to achieve their political goals and to reap astronomical wealth? I shall let the reader decide.

Trump's efforts to help senior citizens afford medicine had to be stopped. Could they do it? They already have. Biden was their man. Upon assuming office, he immediately canceled Trump's executive orders, allowing

---

[6] *http://www.amzn.com/1737478501*

the drug companies to continue using cheap Chinese labor and to keep charging struggling Americans exorbitant drug prices.

The collusion between the Biden administration and Big Pharma to threaten imprisonment, curtail free speech, and generally conspire to increase their own power, is exposed in *Capitol Punishment,* a documentary released in November of 2021 which chronicles how the Biden regime is hunting down and incarcerating Republican Trump supporters. It reveals that the FBI is bashing down doors, handcuffing grandmothers, and dragging innocent citizens off to jail for simply supporting President Trump. Some have been held in solitary confinement for weeks without being allowed to contact their attorneys.

Merely expressing your concern over Marxist indoctrination at your child's school can get you marked as a domestic terrorist by the FBI. The lie that the peaceful protest at the Capitol on January 6th was some sort of insurrection is exposed in this horrifying film. The movie can be purchased here: https://capitolpunishmentthemovie.com and the trailer for the movie can be seen here: https://rumble.com/vpe2o4-capitol-punishment-trailer.html

The attempts of our government to limit free speech and harass anyone the Democratic Party considers a problem has not escaped the notice of the international community. The Russian Foreign Ministry recently issued a statement lambasting the Biden regime for the "ongoing persecution campaign" taking place "against anybody at all who does not agree with the results of the latest presidential election." Their statement reads in part:

"The FBI has reportedly opened more than 400 criminal cases and applied for more than 500 search warrants and subpoenas for suspects; it has also brought charges against and detained around 200 people. Only several dozen

defendants have been released on bail or placed under house arrest. The others are being subjected to harsh pressure, with members of their family and social circle being coerced into giving a 'convenient' testimony. Moreover, people who have not even been officially charged are losing their jobs; they are being banned from social media and publicly ostracised."

The statement continued with a scathing assessment of the human rights situation in the United States under Joe Biden:

"In this context, we have every reason to express concern and demand that basic human rights be observed…US officials are constantly and hypocritically taking care of these rights when it comes to other countries; and yet, they have no scruples in ignoring them at home."

Who would have ever thought that America would degrade to the point that we should be the subject of a human rights lecture by Russia? Imagine if you will, a world where it is considered criminal to discuss the danger of vaccine side effects, where one is branded an insurrectionist for speaking of election irregularities, where political prisoners languish in solitary confinement,[7] where working for a Republican president can get your house searched and yourself hauled away to jail in handcuffs, where displaying an American flag could mark you as a domestic terrorist, where churches are forcibly closed, and children are handcuffed and jailed for not wearing a mask.[8] You don't have to imagine. This is no make-believe dystopia of a fictional future. It is the Orwellian reality of the America we live in today.

---

[7] *BLM rioters and Antifa thugs are off the hook while Trump-supporting, anti-Biden protesters suffer in jail for months, charged with obstruction and other silly crimes. See:* https://amgreatness.com/2021/09/17/joe-bidens-political-prisoners/

[8] https://www.foxnews.com/media/wyoming-high-school-student-arrested-not-wearing-mask

4

Front Line Doctors

In today's apocalyptic reality, Big Pharma has morphed into an uncaring politically-connected machine that is unconcerned about saving lives with existing cheap medicines. If Big Pharma doesn't care, if the government doesn't care, then who does? I will tell you.

A group known as America's Front Line Doctors cares. Who are they? If you google them you will get Big Tech's propaganda – that they are a subversive right-wing political group spreading disinformation. If you have read this far you already understand that you can't necessarily believe anything Big Tech says. The truth is that America's Front Line Doctors are an ever-growing group of hard-working medical doctors on the front lines of the pandemic, treating Covid patients day by day. Here is what they say about themselves:

The doctor-patient relationship is being threatened. That means quality patient care is under fire like never before. Powerful interests are undermining the effective practice of medicine with politicized science and biased information. Now more than ever, patients need access to independent, evidence-based information to make the best decisions for their healthcare. Doctors must have the independence to care for their patients without interference from government, media and the medical establishment...we believe that safe and effective, over-the-counter Covid preventative and early treatment options should be made available to all Americans who need them.[9]

Before the vaccines came out, doctors on the front lines who were caring for the sick were desperate to find a treatment that would save lives. Many of these doctors were not content to just send their patients home to die. They disagreed with the standard of Covid-19 care decreed by the FDA: "Go home, incubate, get sicker, and die if you must, but don't call us until you are seriously ill."

That is not an exaggeration. Sick people with Covid, all over America, were told this. I was. Even though I have five comorbidities and am 66 years old, I was instructed that if I had Covid I was to do nothing but go home until I was sick enough to be at death's door, and even then, I was not to call my doctor, but just go the emergency room and languish in the waiting room.

Fortunately, some courageous doctors have refused to be so careless. They knew good medicine means early treatment. They dared to buck the system, even at personal risk to their careers. These became rebels with a cause. They wanted to save lives, no matter what it cost them personally.

These brave souls fighting on the front lines of the pandemic began searching for medicines that already existed that might help combat the disease. Many of them began prescribing medicines off-label. Trying anything sensible was better than doing nothing. They began comparing notes and observing what doctors in other countries were trying.

One medicine considered was the anti-malarial drug hydroxychloroquine, also known as HCQ or hydroxy for short. This medicine is also used for Lupus. When it was noted that people who had Lupus had a very low incidence

---

[9] *https://thetruthaboutcovid.com/americas-frontline-doctors/*

of Covid, further investigation led to the discovery that hydroxychloroquine, which Lupus sufferers take daily, seemed to be protecting them from getting Covid. Further research revealed that *in-vitro*[10] studies showed hydroxy inhibited the replication of the SARS-CoV-2 virus that causes Covid illness.

Many doctors began using hydroxy and had good success with the drug, particularly when given early and with zinc and azithromycin. This came to the attention of medical researchers on President Trump's Covid task force. President Trump was made aware of the medical research on the drug. He then commented to the news media that hydroxy was a possible therapeutic of great promise. That comment unleashed an avalanche of derision from the left, who were obsessed with debunking anything the President said.

A meeting of the Corona task force was convened in the Situation Room of the White House to discuss using hydroxy. Vice President Mike Pence chaired the meeting. The general consensus was that reports from around the world showed that hydroxy was working and that it was a safe drug with few side effects. It was noted that hydroxy blocks the Covid virus by preventing its spike protein from attaching to ACE-2 cell receptors, thus preventing it from entering cells and replicating. It also combats Covid by virtue of being a zinc ionophore. That means it helps transport zinc through the cell membrane into the cell where it can inhibit the replication of the virus.

It was further noted that hydroxy had been FDA approved and in use for over 60 years, was quite inexpensive and abundant, and had always been deemed safe for even pregnant women and nursing mothers. Peter Navarro, the Defense Production Act coordinator advised

---

[10] *In-Vitro: Test tube studies on microorganisms outside their normal biological context.*

the task force that they had 60 million tablets of hydroxy sitting in FEMA stockpiles ready for immediate delivery across the United States.

Numerous studies had shown that hydroxy was highly effective against Covid if given within the first week of infection, but was not so effective for those who were in later stages of the disease, thus early out-patient treatment was essential for success. **Over three hundred completed studies involving over four thousand scientists studying hydroxy in over four-hundred thousand patients had clearly shown the drug to be safe and effective, reducing death by as much as 75 percent, if given early and administered with zinc and azithromycin.** Remember those stats next time someone tells you there are no studies showing the efficacy of hydroxy against Covid.

During the meeting, Surgeon General Jerome Adams commented that hydroxy certainly can't hurt you and that there seemed to be evidence that it could help. Doctor Stephen Hagn, M.D. from the FDA agreed. All was going well and soon there would be an inexpensive life-saving pill that people could take as soon as they were diagnosed with Covid, or so it seemed.

But sad to say, there was a mad scientist at the table of that meeting. He was of another persuasion and had his own agenda. The Dalai Lama of Big Pharma and the prima donna darling of the Democratic Party was poised to derail the hydroxy train.

5

Doctor Von Fauci-Stein

If you thought mad scientists such as Doctor Frankenstein were merely figments of science fiction you would be mistaken. The label certainly exists in the minds of those who have come to disdain a public figure whose actions have brought increasing suspicion and derision from the populace.

Doctor Anthony Fauci is an immunologist serving as the director of the National Institute of Allergy and Infectious Diseases (NIAID), a part of the NIH. He has been the Chief Medical Advisor to several presidents, including President Trump, who inherited his services from previous administrations. Like many in the deep state, he has not declared his party affiliation, an advantageous practice common among those who serve under both Republican and Democrat administrations. Nevertheless, it is common knowledge that Dr. Fauci is a leftist. He contributed financially, through his wife's name, to Hillary Clinton's campaign against Donald Trump.

Dr. Fauci is the highest-paid federal employee in America, making almost half a million dollars a year, raking in a tax-supported salary even higher than that of the president. Fauci has become quite a media figure as he has enjoyed the popularity of appearing on numerous liberal news outlets and talk shows where he has delighted himself in contradicting President Trump and pompously lecturing the American people about modifying their behavior. He has been particularly fond of discouraging church attendance and has cautioned against singing in church.

Yet, while being interviewed for a Vanity Fair article, Fauci was asked about the feasibility of people hooking up with a "hot" stranger from the Internet during the Covid pandemic. Fauci responded, *"You could figure out if you want to meet somebody...If you want to go...intimate, well, then that's your choice..."*

Later in the interview, Fauci declared, *"I don't think we should ever shake hands ever again..."* This begs the question, what sort of mind approves the government closing of churches, supports a permanent ban on shaking hands, but then muses that fornicating in a one-night sexual rendezvous with a stranger could be an acceptable personal choice during a pandemic?

Other unsavory facts have recently surfaced which reflect on Fauci's character and judgment. Fauci strongly opposed President Trump's travel ban on flights from China, saying that there was no danger from the Covid virus. We know now how wrong Fauci was and how right Trump was.

What has not been as well known is that Fauci was and is involved in cruel experiments upon puppies wherein their heads were enclosed in cages filled with disease-infected sand flies to see if an injection they had been given had efficacy. But first, the puppy's vocal cords were ripped out so researchers would not have to hear the puppies yelp, whine, and cry in agony.

When they were done torturing the poor animals, they killed and dissected them. PETA[11] has stated,

"Anthony Fauci and all the NIH directors have defended a cruel, archaic system for far too long. It's time for them to get out of the way and let modern scientists take over...our position is clear. ALL those in leadership at NIH, including Fauci, should resign,"

---

[11] *PETA – People for Ethical Treatment of Animals*

In the footnote, you will find a link to a graphic video of what people are calling the Fauci torture chamber.[12]

It has also come to light that Fauci used his position at the NIH to provide 3.7 million dollars in funding to the bio-weapons lab in Wuhan for gain-of-function research on bat corona viruses. Think about that. Fauci gave millions in tax-payer dollars to a biological weapons laboratory in Communist China that was under the authority of the Chinese Military. That money was used to modify bat viruses to make them more capable of infecting humans.

Years earlier, gain-of-function research had been expressly forbidden by the Obama administration due to some close calls that had occurred in our own laboratories. In violation of that decree, Fauci stealthily managed to do this anyway without the knowledge of the Trump administration. Somewhere inside his twisted mind, he thought it would be safer to pay our enemies to do this dangerous work in their bio-weapons laboratory.

Dr. Fauci then lied to Congress about his culpability in the matter. His duplicity was discovered when a piece of communication was discovered from Dr. Shi Zhengli, the Wuhan Institute of Virology's "Bat Woman," wherein she thanked the U.S. National Institutes of Health, headed by Dr. Fauci, for their contribution in gain-of-function research on bat viruses. Shi Zhengli even acknowledged Dr. Fauci's personal support in her published research papers.

Today there is no question that the coronavirus did come from the Wuhan lab. A Congressional investigation by the House Foreign Affairs Committee has unequivocally

---

[12] *https://sputniknews.com/20211025/video-showing-puppy-experiments-overseen-by-fauci-goes-viral-amid-online-campaign-to-arrest-him-1090190166.html*

concluded that *"the preponderance of evidence proves that the virus did leak"* from the Wuhan laboratory.[13]

Following is the transcript of a Senate hearing conducted on July 20, 2021, where Senator Rand Paul, himself also a medical doctor, questions Dr. Fauci (NIAID director of the NIH) under oath. Note how desperately, yet ineffectively, Dr. Fauci tries to evade the truth of his culpability in the creation of the virus.

Senator Paul:

Dr. Fauci, as you are aware, it is a crime to lie to Congress. Section 1.0.0.1 of the U.S. Criminal Code creates a felony and a five-year penalty for lying to Congress. On your last trip to our committee on May 11th, you stated that the NIH has not ever, and does not now, fund gain-of-function research in the Wuhan Institute of Virology. And yet, gain-of-function research was done entirely in the Wuhan Institute by Dr. Shi and was funded by the NIH.

I'd like to ask for unanimous consent to insert into the record the Wuhan virology paper entitled Discovery of a Rich Gene Pool of Bat SARS Related coronaviruses. Please deliver a copy of the journal article to Dr. Fauci.

In this paper, Dr. Shi credits the NIH and lists the actual number of the grant that she was given by the NIH. In this paper, she took two bat coronavirus genes, spike genes, and combined them with a SARS-related backbone to create new viruses that are not found in nature. These lab-created viruses were then to shown to replicate in humans. These experiments combined genetic information from different coronaviruses that infect animals, but not humans, to create novel artificial viruses able to infect human cells.

---

[13] https://www.taiwannews.com.tw/en/news/4267712

Viruses that in nature only infect animals were manipulated in the Wuhan lab to gain the function of infecting humans. This research fits the definition of the research that the NIH said was subject to the pause in 2014 to 2017, a pause in funding on gain-of-function, but the NIH failed to recognize this, defines it away, and it never came under any scrutiny.

Dr. Richard Ebright, a molecular biologist from Rutgers, described this research in Wuhan as, "the Wuhan lab used NIH funding to construct novel chimeric SARS related to coronaviruses able to infect human cells and laboratory animals."

This is high-risk research that creates new potential pandemic pathogens, potential pandemic pathogens that exist only in the lab, not in nature. This research matches – these are Dr. Ebright's words – this research matches, indeed epitomizes the definition of gain-of-function research, done entirely in Wuhan, for which there was supposed to be a federal pause.

Dr. Fauci, knowing that it is a crime to lie to Congress, do you wish to retract your statement of May 11th, where you claimed that the NIH never funded gain-of-function research in Wuhan?

Dr. Fauci:

Senator Paul, I have never lied before the Congress, and I do not retract that statement. This paper that you were referring to was judged by qualified staff up and down the chain as not being gain-of-function.

Senator Paul:

You take an animal virus and you increase its transmissibility to humans. You're saying that's not gain-of-function?

Dr. Fauci:

Yeah, that is correct... And Senator Paul, you do not know what you are talking about, quite frankly. And I want to say that officially, you do not know what you are talking about, okay?

Senator Paul:

This is your definition that you guys wrote. It says that scientific research that increases the transmissibility among animals is gain-of-function. They took animal viruses that only occur in animals, and they increased their transmissibility to humans. How can you say that is not gain-of-function?

Dr. Fauci:

It is not.

Senator Paul:

It's a dance, and you're dancing around this because you're trying to obscure responsibility for 4 million people dying around the world from a pandemic...all the evidence is pointing that it came from the lab, and there will be responsibility for those who funded the lab, including yourself.

Dr. Fauci is quickly rescued from this confrontation by his Democrat colleagues who ask him to talk about the importance of universal vaccination. Bear in mind as we go through this, that Dr. Fauci has never treated a Covid patient himself. He is a research scientist, a political bureaucrat, and a member of Big Pharma, but first and foremost, he is a political hack of the Democratic Party who hates President Trump.

Just so everyone makes the connection, I will state it plainly. Dr. Fauci, in contradiction to federal policy, illicitly gave hard-earned tax dollars of the American people to a bio-weapons laboratory of the Chinese Communist Party to be used to modify and weaponize the corona bat virus that was eventually loosed upon the world. Then He lied about it to Congress, under oath. It doesn't get any more "mad scientist" than that. Actually, it does. Back to our meeting at the White House. Doctor Von Fauci-Stein is about to derail plans that many doctors believe would have saved hundreds of thousands of lives.

6

Sinister Sabotage

Now let us return to the Situation Room of the White House where widespread early use of hydroxychloroquine is about to be unanimously approved for distribution across America so that doctors can immediately begin prescribing it for use in the early treatment of Covid. Suddenly Dr. Fauci spoke up, claiming that there was "only anecdotal evidence" for the efficacy of hydroxy and that there were no real scientific studies to show that it worked.

Peter Navarro, the Defense Production Act coordinator was prepared for this. He had seen Dr. Fauci, time and again, stand against common-sense measures to protect the American people. From opposing flight restrictions from China to challenging Trump's questioning of the accuracy of Covid death numbers, Anthony Fauci had demonstrated a petty propensity for contradicting anything that Trump said.

President Trump had publicly stated, based upon what doctors had told him, that he believed hydroxy may hold great promise. Consequently, Peter Navarro thought Fauci might oppose hydroxy, if for no other reason than because the president had said he believed it worked. What happened next after Fauci's "only anecdotal evidence" statement is best told by Peter Navarro himself:

Immediately, I stood up from my backbench chair just behind Vice President Pence and walked straight toward Fauci. As I approached him, I saw fear in his eyes. I'm sure it crossed his mind that I might physically assault him.

Instead, I dumped my large dossier of studies onto the table in front of him and said to Fauci as much as to everyone else in the room—especially VPOTUS—

"Tony, these are not anecdotes. That's more than fifty scientific studies in support of hydroxy. Fifty! So stop spouting your crap about there only being anecdotal evidence because not only is it counterfactual, you are going to kill people just like you did during the AIDS crisis when you refused to approve medicines that everybody but you knew worked." [14]

To make a long story short, some irregular anomalies occurred after this meeting – things that have led many to believe that Dr. Fauci went to his powerful contacts in Big Pharma and pulled the strings necessary to totally kill the use of hydroxy. In short order, out of nowhere came studies that showed hydroxy was dangerous and did not work against Covid.

For example, a French study suddenly came to light that showed hydroxy was ineffective, but an important fact was hidden from the public – that study was done on people in the final stages of Covid. Hydroxy only works if given early, [15] when a person first gets sick. So of course, this study showed no efficacy for hydroxy.

Then there was a Brazilian study that showed hydroxy killed patients. What was hidden was the fact that the drug was again given to people in the final stages of the disease, and that one group consisted of patients over 75 who were viewed as most likely to die, while the other group had younger patients. The younger patient group was given a small dose of hydroxy but the older group was overdosed with "enough medicine to bring an elephant to its knees." [16]

---

[14] *Navarro, Peter. In Trump Time: A Journal of America's Plague Year (pp. 97-98). All Seasons Press.*

[15] *And in conjunction with zinc and azithromycin.*

[16] *Navarro, Peter. In Trump Time: A Journal of America's Plague Year (p. 99). All Seasons Press. Kindle Edition.*

No wonder that the older group who were overdosed had side effects and more deaths.

If you want the long story, I highly recommend Peter Navarro's book, *In Trump Time* where he tells the entire sordid story of how Dr. Fauci appears to have used his connections to lash back against anyone who dared disagree with him. Flawed and biased studies, like those mentioned above, were quickly released to the liberal mass news media who were only too happy to report that "science" had proved President Trump wrong.

CNN and other voices of the Democratic Party immediately began gleefully proclaiming loudly and repeatedly that "President Trump's hydroxychloroquine" was a dangerous drug that has no effect on Covid whatsoever. Social media and Big Tech fell into lockstep with the message. Even today, you can google "Will hydroxychloroquine work against Covid" and you will find the search results will be pages of links to articles that say it is not effective. If you try to post any real scientific facts about hydroxy on Facebook or YouTube, your post will be quickly banned. This collusion between Big Pharma, Big Tech, and a Democratically controlled Congress that attempts to silence the populace are an infringement on freedom of speech.

As a result of Fauci's opposition, the FDA took a strong position against hydroxy. The use of a medicine that, in the opinion of many medical doctors, if given early would have saved hundreds of thousands of lives, was stopped in its tracks. One wonders, did all this happen just because Dr. Fauci got his feelings hurt and because he wanted to undermine President Trump, or is something more sinister at play?

One must remember that Big Pharma was in hot pursuit of inventing a new drug that would make them trillions of dollars. If it were to be discovered that there was an existing generic drug that was extremely cheap and effective, their dreams of profit would be dashed. There was simply no serious money to be made from a cheap existing drug such as hydroxychloroquine.

The pharmaceutical company known as Gilead Sciences was working on a new drug called remdesivir. It was less effective compared to hydroxy and would be inconvenient for the patient, as it must be administered by IV. But it had one advantage that hydroxy didn't have. Remdesivir would sell for thousands of dollars per treatment, providing the manufacturer with huge profit margins.

Is it really that hard to imagine that there might be nameless faces of powerful people in various drug companies who would not have much interest in cheap medicine already on the shelves? Imagine you are the CEO of a company that invents a new expensive drug that everyone in the world needs. Envision it is your company that saves the world. Picture yourself daydreaming of the new multi-million-dollar yacht you are going to buy for your family. If you can pull it off, there would be trillions of dollars to spread around to grease the skids of government and media, or wherever needed, to make sure the profit train doesn't ever get derailed by pesky doctors saying they found something that works, something cheap, abundant, low-profit margin and with an expired patent. To keep the gravy train on track all you need to do is provide financial incentive to certain politicians, news agencies, and social media platforms so they will be inspired to squelch the inconvenient truth of a cheap cure.

There is another caveat to consider which explains the suspicious actions of Big Pharma. Any new medicine to come out, whether a vaccine or a novel therapeutic, would need to be released under what is called an "Emergency Use Authorization" from the FDA. Otherwise, it could take years to get it through full FDA approval. Now here is the point: The law specifies that an Emergency Use Authorization cannot be issued if there is an existing remedy that is effective. Here is what the law says:

21 U.S.C. § 360bbb-3 - U.S. Code

"The Secretary may issue an authorization under this section with respect to the emergency use of a product only if...there is no adequate, approved, and available alternative to the product for diagnosing, preventing, or treating such disease or condition."[17]

So, if any medicine such as hydroxy were to be found effective, there could be no Emergency Use Authorization given. The new drug would then have to go through the normal manner of investigation for safety as required by the FDA, which could take years. Once the vaccines came close to coming out, Big Pharma had an even stronger incentive to squelch any existing drug from being discovered as effective, for it would negate the grounds for their petition to the FDA for an Emergency Use Authorization for the novel mRNA vaccines.

So, was there more going on than Fauci's toes getting stepped on? Did powerful political forces want to make President Trump look bad? Was it drug companies pursuing the almighty dollar in disregard for saving lives? Was it all three? Let the reader decide, but just in case someone is naïve enough to believe there are not powerful narcissistic people in the world willing to let others die for the sake of their personal gain, then consider what Peter Navarro wrote after he noticed Fauci's strange manipulation of research data:

"When I heard about that, I found it just plain weird. At least I found it weird until Doc Hatfill told me to follow the

---

[17] https://codes.findlaw.com/us/title-21-food-and-drugs/21-usc-sect-360bbb-3.html

money. And as it always is with Fauci, the money trail leads directly back to Fauci's patron saint, Big Pharma, an industry that has helped make Fauci the highest-paid bureaucrat in the entire US government."[18]

The fact remains that the science supports hydroxy. Don't take my word for it. Hear what Doctor Hatfill says. Dr. Steven Hatfill is a specialist physician and a virologist with a military background and separate master's degrees in microbial genetics, radiation biochemistry, and experimental pathology. His medical fellowships include Oxford University, the NIH in Bethesda, and the NRC where he studied the Ebola Virus at the US Army Institute for Infectious Diseases at Fort Detrick. He worked with the president's task force to combat Corona. After Dr. Fauci's ambush of hydroxy, Dr. Hatfill shook his head sadly and said to Peter Navarro:

"India's population is five times larger than that of the United States, but India's death toll has been only about thirty percent of America's. The difference is India's widespread use of hydroxychloroquine both as a prophylactic and in early-treatment use."[19]

In the face of the mountains of evidence and studies that show hydroxychloroquine works against Covid, what excuse do doctors give for not prescribing it? I can tell you what my doctor said: "The best studies, the gold standard, are American studies that are double-blind, randomized, placebo-controlled trials. Unless it is that kind of study, we don't ascribe much weight to it."

Sounds official. What is left unsaid is that other countries have smart doctors to. Other countries have clinical studies which are extremely revealing. When a doctor uses hydroxy to treat a thousand patients with

---

[18] *Navarro, Peter. In Trump Time: A Journal of America's Plague Year (p. 86). All Seasons Press. Kindle Edition.*
[19] *Navarro, Peter. In Trump Time: A Journal of America's Plague Year (pp. 109-110). All Seasons Press. Kindle Edition.*

comorbidities for Covid and doesn't lose one, that says something. When that same scenario repeats for other doctors, that has weight. When entire regions that take hydroxy are protected from Covid, that has merit. Establishment doctors scratch their heads at that and say, "Well, we need a gold-standard study to be sure about it. Then we will know." In the meanwhile, people are dying. The problem is this: It is drug companies that dish out the millions of dollars needed for that kind of study. They are not going to do that for hydroxy. Its patent has expired. There is no money in it for them.

You might be thinking that this book is about hydroxychloroquine and that it is the "cure" that is the subject of this book. You would be mistaken. Although hydroxy is effective if given early, another medicine was discovered later that is much more effective, and not just when given early, but provides benefit at any stage of the disease.

This other medicine is far more effective than hydroxy, while at the same time being just as cheap and safe. Unfortunately, a disinformation campaign was launched against it that is every bit as suspicious, diabolical, and unfair as that which was rained down on hydroxychloroquine.

7

Ivermectin

Laura-Lynn Tyler Thompson made her way into the hospital with a prayer on her lips and contraband in her purse. Inside the hospital was her eighty-six-year-old father, languishing in intensive care with a severe case of Covid pneumonia. Nurses had told her that he was not expected to live. He was nearly gone. She had been advised to come and say her goodbyes.

Laura made her way to the Intensive Care Unit. At her father's bedside, she lovingly fed and cared for her aging father. When she was alone, she carefully looked around to see if anyone was watching. Earlier she had begged the doctors to give her father a drug called ivermectin. They had refused, so after prayer and careful consideration, she had decided to take matters into her own hands. Cautiously she opened her purse and retrieved the forbidden medicine, giving her dad both ivermectin and hydroxychloroquine. She secretly continued this for a few days while her dad began to improve so quickly that it surprised the doctors. Within a matter of days, Laura was able to take her father home, fully recovered from Covid.

How Ivermectin for Covid was Discovered

Researchers in America discovered that the incidence of Covid in some African countries was unusually low, almost non-existent compared to other countries. What was protecting them? The population of these countries had for some time been given ivermectin to be taken continually as a prophylactic measure to prevent infection with a parasite that causes a disease known as river blindness. It was suspected that it was this routine mass administration of ivermectin for parasite control that had protected the populace from Covid.

Researchers intensified their study of African countries that have wide use of ivermectin. They divided Africa between countries that have ivermectin programs for control of river blindness and those that don't. The countries without ivermectin programs had 4.3 times more cases and 5.7 times more Covid deaths despite having a 220,000,000 smaller population.

60 AFRICA Daily DEATHS/100K, Ivermectin Countries vs Non-Ivermectin Countries: A Picture is worth a THOUSAND JABS!

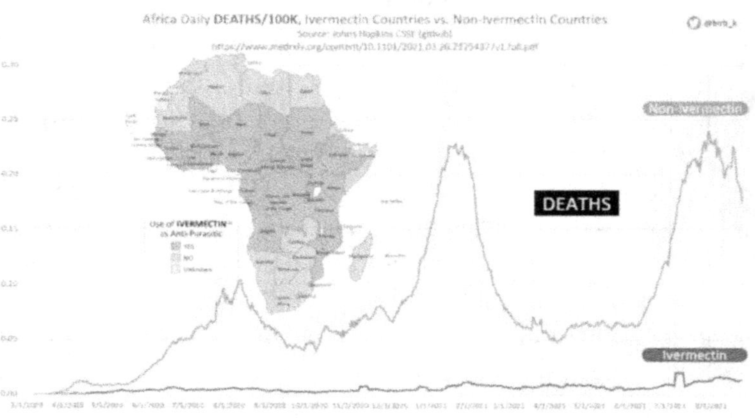

The top line of this graph shows Covid deaths in African countries not using ivermectin. The bottom line shows Covid deaths in countries where the populace took ivermectin regularly – talk about "flattening the curve!" Ivermectin flattened it into the ground. Imagine the lives that could have been saved if ivermectin had been put to use everywhere. Envision it – no lockdowns, no masks, no business or school closures. All that could have been avoided.

Now imagine the trillions of dollars that would not be made by Big Pharma if ivermectin had been used. Now you understand. For some people, money and power matter more than lives.

And it was not just Africa where ivermectin saved lives. Studies of states in India gave the same conclusion. In the states of Delhi, Uttar Pradesh, Uttarakhand, and Goa where ivermectin was widely used as a preventative against Covid, cases declined by 98%, 97%, 94%, and 86% respectively.

In Argentina, a study was conducted with twelve hundred healthcare works by Dr. Hector E. Carvallo to see if ivermectin could protect against infection with Covid. Four hundred healthcare workers received no ivermectin and two hundred thirty-seven of them contracted Covid, a 58% infection rate. The other eight hundred healthcare workers were given a steady dose of ivermectin. Not one single healthcare worker taking ivermectin contracted Covid, a 0% infection rate. In other words, this study showed that ivermectin was 100% effective in protecting against Covid.

If hydroxy was a godsend, ivermectin was a miracle cure on steroids sent from heaven. Its effectiveness exceeded that of hydroxychloroquine. This barely touches the surface of the plethora of scientific studies showing the efficacy of ivermectin for Covid patients. For those who want to read more studies, I recommend flccc.net where one can peruse mountains of evidence concerning ivermectin efficacy against Covid and its stellar safety record.

Ivermectin is an FDA-approved drug that came into use in 1981. It is cheap, safe, and widely available. It has been given more than 3.7 billion times around the world with very few side effects reported in its years of usage. It has been mainly used for parasites in humans but is also used in animals for the same purpose.

As news of the ability of ivermectin to quash Covid, Big Pharma went into full alert, ramping up their propaganda machine. The liberal fake news media condescendingly denigrated the drug, calling it "horse medicine." The fact that it is also used in animals is a moot point. Yes, it is also used in animals but then so is penicillin. Certainly, no one would call penicillin horse medicine. Many medications intended for human use are also given to animals.

The liberal news media derides anyone taking ivermectin, belittling them for taking "horse de-wormer." But as a point of fact, ivermectin has secretly been the first choice for members of Congress. Dr. Pierre Kory from the *Front Line Critical Care Covid Alliance*, says that he has privately treated over two-hundred members of Congress with ivermectin.[20]

This wonderful medicine has been prescribed for humans for decades. It does a lot more than just kill parasites. It has been found to have both anti-inflammatory and antiviral properties, demonstrating broad-spectrum antiviral activity against many viruses including HIV, ZIKA, and MERS.

Doctors have recently discovered that ivermectin can inhibit the spike protein of the coronavirus from binding to cell receptors, thus preventing it from entering cells and thereby stopping its replication. Additionally, its powerful anti-inflammatory properties can prevent the cytokine storm that is one of the ways Covid kills.

The Website of the *Front Line COVID-19 Critical Care Alliance* is the mouthpiece of doctors who have been on the

---

[20]*https://www.realclearpolitics.com/video/2021/10/26/joe_rogan_says_dr_pierre_kory _treated_200_members_of_congress_with_ivermectin.html*

front line fighting Covid by caring for infected patients. They have this to say about ivermectin:

"It is one of the safest drugs known. It is on the WHO's list of essential medicines, has been given 3.7 billion times around the globe, and has won the Nobel prize for its global and historic impacts in eradicating endemic parasitic infections in many parts of the world. Our medical discovery of a rapidly growing published medical evidence base, demonstrating ivermectin's unique and highly potent ability to inhibit SARS-CoV-2 replication and to suppress inflammation, prompted our team to use ivermectin for prevention and treatment in all stages of COVID-19."[21]

The FDA War Against Ivermectin

Ivermectin would be destructive to the profits of Big Pharma. Like hydroxy, ivermectin's patent has expired and thus it has no major profit potential. The FDA has declared war on ivermectin. They have an entire page on their website that is designed to scare people away from using it.[22] It is filled with obfuscation and misinformation. Let's take a look at a couple examples. Here is what they say:

When can taking ivermectin be unsafe? The FDA has not authorized or approved ivermectin for the treatment or prevention of COVID-19 in people or animals. Ivermectin has not been shown to be safe or effective for these indications.

So, the FDA says it is unsafe to take a prescription of ivermectin if you have Covid. That is a lie. There is overwhelming evidence that doctor-prescribed ivermectin

---

[21] https://covid19criticalcare.com/ivermectin-in-covid-19/

[22] https://www.fda.gov/consumers/consumer-updates/why-you-should-not-use-ivermectin-treat-or-prevent-covid-19

is not only safe but has saved the lives of many Covid patients. The website goes on to say:

You can also overdose on ivermectin, which can cause nausea, vomiting, diarrhea, hypotension (low blood pressure), allergic reactions (itching and hives), dizziness, ataxia (problems with balance), seizures, coma and even death.

Well, yea – if you overdose. Duh! You can overdose on acetaminophen and kill yourself too. Does that mean you should not take acetaminophen for a headache? Of course not. Ivermectin is safe when taken as directed by a physician. The FDA concludes their page with:

Talk to your health care provider about available COVID-19 vaccines.

Aha! There it is – that is their bottom line. The whole point of their page on ivermectin is to sell more vaccines and that means killing ivermectin, regardless of how many people die as a result. To sell vaccines you need people to be more afraid of the virus than they are of the vaccine. If ivermectin is a viable option, the requisite fear will not be engendered.

The CDC gets in on the act too with web pages dedicated to discouraging the use of ivermectin.[23] They have an article with a big bold scary title: *"Severe Illness Associated with Use of Products Containing ivermectin."* But the examples they give have nothing to do with taking ivermectin for humans that is prescribed by a doctor. For example, their page includes scary stories like this:

An adult drank an injectable ivermectin formulation intended for use in cattle in an attempt to prevent COVID-19 infection. This patient presented to a hospital with confusion, drowsiness, visual hallucinations, tachypnea,

---

[23] *https://emergency.cdc.gov/han/2021/han00449.asp*

and tremors. The patient recovered after being hospitalized for nine days.

An adult patient presented with altered mental status after taking ivermectin tablets of unknown strength purchased on the internet. The patient reportedly took five tablets a day for five days to treat COVID-19. The patient was disoriented and had difficulty answering questions and following commands. Symptoms improved with discontinuation of ivermectin after hospital admission.

Of course, bad things are going to happen when people who have no clue what they are doing take ivermectin for animals from unknown sources with no guidance. You will note that even in these extreme examples, the patients recovered completely from their foolish overdose with the big bad drug. Worse than this happens with acetaminophen all the time, yet we don't see Big Pharma launching a disinformation campaign against acetaminophen.

But who's fault is all this foolishness? It is the fault of the FDA, the CDC, and all of Big Pharma. They are the ones that have tried to prevent doctors from prescribing ivermectin to patients. They are the ones who ignore and denigrate all the studies and clinical evidence which show that ivermectin works. They are the ones who have made it difficult to get an ivermectin prescription. That is what has caused people to engage in this unsafe behavior. It is their fault. All of it.

In July of 2021, the Wall Street Journal published an article questioning the tactics of the FDA regarding ivermectin.[24] The link is in the footnote and I encourage the reader to peruse the entire article. It reads in part:

The Food and Drug Administration claims to follow the science. So why is it attacking ivermectin, a medication it

---

[24]   *https://covid19criticalcare.com/wp-content/uploads/2021/07/Why-Is-the-FDA-Attacking-a-Safe-Effective-Drug_-WSJ.pdf*

certified in 1996? Earlier this year the agency put out a special warning that "you should not use ivermectin to treat or prevent COVID-19." The FDA's statement included words and phrases such as "serious harm," "hospitalized," "dangerous," "very dangerous," "seizures," "coma and even death" and "highly toxic." Any reader would think the FDA was warning against poison pills. In fact, the drug is FDA-approved as a safe and effective antiparasitic... Moreover, the drug can help prevent Covid-19."

Dr. Pierre Kory wrote an excellent article delineating the war on ivermectin.[25] I recommend everyone read this article as well. It reads in part:

Doctors fighting COVID-19 should be supported by their profession and their government, not suppressed. Yet today physicians are smothered under a wave of censorship. With coronavirus variants and vaccine hesitancy threatening a prolonged pandemic, the National Institutes of Health and the broader U.S. medical establishment should free doctors to treat this terrible disease with effective medicines.

For centuries, doctors have addressed emerging health threats by prescribing existing drugs for new uses, observing the results, and communicating to their peers and the public what seems to work. In a pandemic, precious time and lives can be lost by an insistence on excessive data and review. But in the current crisis, many in positions of authority have done just that, stubbornly refusing to allow any repurposed treatments. This departure from traditional medical practice risks catastrophe. When doctors on the front lines try to bring awareness of and use such medicines, they get silenced.

---

[25] *https://www.realclearpolitics.com/articles/2021/03/10/censorship_kills_the_shunning_of_a_covid_therapeutic_145376.html*

Testimonials

There are literally tens of thousands of people that testify to the life-saving effects of taking ivermectin for Covid. Here are just a couple:

In Buffalo, New York, attorney Ralph Lorigo received a call from a family whose 80-year-old mother was in a hospital hooked up to a ventilator. She was dying and the family wanted her to be given ivermectin, but the hospital refused. Lorigo procured a court order from a judge that ordered the hospital to administer ivermectin. In less than a week, after receiving ivermectin the mother's condition dramatically improved and she was soon able to go home.[26]

When 57-year-old Patti Koopmans came down with Covid she developed a fever of nearly 103 degrees. She felt absolutely miserable, with vomiting and diarrhea. Her doctor called in a prescription of ivermectin, but the pharmacy only had a partial dose available. She took that and within eight hours of taking that partial dose, she was markedly improved. In Patti's words:

Eight hours after my partial dose I felt 100% better! My appetite returned, and no temperature or nausea. It was like a miracle![27]

A short video describing her experience is in the footnote. I also recommend the reader visit this page:

https://covid19criticalcare.com/testimonials/

There you will find numerous videos of people testifying to how ivermectin saved their lives or the lives of their loved ones. In the magazine State of the Nation, journalist Nadya Swart puts it succinctly:

---

[26] https://spectrumlocalnews.com/nys/buffalo/politics/2021/09/15/wny-attorney-taking-on-ivermectin-cases-across-the-country

[27] https://odysee.com/@FrontlineCovid19CriticalCareAlliance:c/only-8-hours-after-this-covid-19-patient:f

The calls of medical professionals for ivermectin to be used for the prevention and treatment of Covid-19 have reached desperate levels. An article by Professor Colleen Aldous, published on BizNews.com this week, argued that the placement of our trust in a small group of experts who advocate against ivermectin is being done at the potential cost of human life. Considering the devastation that South Africa has endured due to Covid-19 and the resultant lockdown regulations – it seems absurd not to explore all and any viable alternatives to Covid-19 vaccination in order to best manage the pandemic's merciless grip. This article, written by eleven doctors and professors to the Department of Health, urges the Department to facilitate the use of ivermectin in the public health sector. The article was delivered to President Cyril Ramaphosa's house by Jeremy Gordon who believes that we could end the crisis of the pandemic with the use of ivermectin as they have in Zimbabwe...Indian states that adopted ivermectin policies saw their cases fall far more than 80%...The bottom line is that ivermectin works, and it works extraordinarily well. You do not need to be a scientist to understand these numbers, as they are self-evident.[28]

The loss of life incurred from refusal of the medical establishment to use ivermectin is horrific, yet there is something that may be far worse – the use of dangerous new drugs that are not fully FDA approved. In Greek mythology Pandora opened a box she had no business opening, and thereby released upon the world sickness, death and all manner of evil. To Pandora's horror she found that once these evils escaped into the world, it was impossible to once again contain them. In the next chapter we explore how the mad scientists of Big Pharma are, figuratively speaking, prying open Pandora's box.

---

[28] https://stateofthenation.co/?p=83300

8

My Covid Experience

After standing in a long line, I was finally seated at a table where the nurse prepared to give me my second Covid vaccine. I was very happy to be getting this. They told me the injection was safe and effective and that it would prevent me from ever getting Covid.

I didn't know they were repeating lies. By that evening the shot had done its dastardly deed to my body. I was deathly ill. I lay in bed for three weeks, too sick to do anything more than drag myself to the bathroom when necessary.

Then something happened that I had never experienced in my life. My neck became paralyzed. I could not turn my head even a half-inch in any direction. This was very painful and extremely frightening. My wife had to drive me to the emergency room, as driving myself in this condition would have been impossible. Several days of painkillers and powerful anti-inflammatories and the paralysis gradually subsided. Yet, years later I still have stiffness and limited motion in my neck that I never had before.

Did the vaccine stop me from getting Covid, as they had promised? No, they lied about that too. In point of fact, I've had Covid twice after getting the vaccine. One of my doctors told me they see just as many vaccinated people with Covid as unvaccinated.

Was my Covid sickness less severe because of the vaccine? That is what they claim. Doctors and nurses now confidently tell the vaccinated, "if you get Covid it will be less severe." They say it because the manufacturer of the vaccine has told them this is so, but is it?

There are no studies which prove it to my satisfaction. Think about it – how would they know? According to WebMD.com there are over 50 Covid variants and at any one time nine of them are in circulation, each one with its own symptoms and level of severity. Consider also that everyone's immune system responds differently. So, there is really no way to test or measure the level of sickness of one person compared to what would have been if not vaccinated. Any studies they have on that would be highly suspect and likely be weighted in favor of results that would benefit Big Pharma.

Some unvaccinated people get Covid and barely feel sick at all. I think their claim that the vaccine reduces symptoms may be nothing more than sales jargon. After being lied to about its efficacy and safety, I choose not to believe their assertions or studies anymore – studies that are funded by the manufacturer of the vaccine. I think their claims are designed to defend their vaccine when it fails to prevent Covid. I had two vaccinations and got Covid twice, and I was pretty sick each time for several weeks. And the sickness I had from the vaccine was way worse than having Covid. No more jabs for me.

Vaccination Injury

I am not the only one to claim injury from the vaccine. The Covid vaccine is unlike any other vaccine. It is a new experimental vaccine that uses mRNA technology. How many people have been adversely affected by the vaccine? The FDA Adverse Event Reporting System (FAERS reports many thousands of Covid vaccine injuries every year.

According to the Center for Disease Control (CDC) the vaccinations can lead to:

- ✓ Thrombosis with thrombocytopenia syndrome
- ✓ Myocarditis and pericarditis (inflammation of the heart)
- ✓ Guillain-Barré Syndrome

The FLCCC Alliance is a network of medical doctors who have devoted themselves to helping Covid sufferers as well as those injured by the Covid vaccine. Their website says:

*"Most serious adverse events following vaccination occur in the two weeks immediately following a dose of the vaccine. However, evolving data suggest that some patients who otherwise had no adverse events from the vaccine appear to have delayed acute cardiac events **(often leading to sudden death)**. This appears to peak between 4 to 6 months after the vaccine but may extend for at least one year. There has also been evidence of an emergence of 'turbo' and relapsed cancers in the months following vaccination."*

You can read more about curing Covid and Covid vaccine injury at their website. The link is: www.flccc.net

Ivermectin Saved Me

When I came down with Covid I was prepared. I had home test kits and within a day of feeling ill I tested myself and knew I had Covid. I had ivermectin and zinc on hand and I took it immediately. I began to recover almost immediately.

My wife came down with Covid at about the same time. At first, she didn't want to take the ivermectin. She steadily got worse and felt pretty miserable. Finally, she decided to take the ivermectin. Within hours she was feeling better and she commented, *"This stuff is amazing! It is a real game-changer!"*

The second time I got Covid, I was out of ivermectin. I took Hydroxychloroquine instead, and I quickly began to recover. I have had many family members come down with Covid and they used ivermectin as well. My daughter said she felt remarkably better within the first hour. Forty-five minutes after taking it her appetite and sense of smell returned. Her daughter, who was also sick had the same experience. I have seen these wonderous results play out over and over again with people I know.

9

How to Get Ivermectin

You can ask your local doctor if he is willing to prescribe ivermectin for Covid but that is likely a waste of time. He probably will not do it. If he is willing, ask for it immediately so you can have it on hand if you get Covid. You don't how things might change in the future, so get it now while you still can. When you ask, you are likely to be told that ivermectin doesn't work for Covid. You know better. Your doctor may be a fine healthcare practitioner, but he could be powerfully influenced by whatever Big Pharma tells him. If he turns you down then it is time for you to get a second opinion from another doctor.

As of right now getting ivermectin is easy if you know what hoops to jump through. Here is what you do. This is legal and gets you a prescription from an American doctor filled by an American pharmacy. Go to https://www.pushhealth.com Sign up for an account. You can also install the app on your smartphone. Here are the specific steps to take to get your ivermectin.

1. On a computer, go to Pushhealth.com.
2. Enter name & email.
3. Check the box that you are not a medical provider.
4. Click Get Started.
5. Click Find a Provider.
6. Under Medications, click on ivermectin
7. Click Request Now.
8. Choose the state where you reside.
9. Under Choose Pharmacy, Enter Zip code: 54140.

10. Click Search.

11. Choose Smith Pharmacy in Little Chute, Wisconsin.

12. Enter Patient Health Information.

13. In the Medication Desired field type "ivermectin."

14. For Quantity and Dosage enter a question mark.

15. Reason: Enter, "Want ivermectin in case I contract Covid."

16. Enter weight accurately – your dosage is based on that.

17. Click on Submit Request.

18. Enter payment details.

19. Choose No Preference on selecting a provider.

20. You will see: Medical provider matching in Process.

21. Follow any prompts given.

22. Keep an eye on your email for messages.

23. Monitor messages on the website or phone app.

24. Call pharmacy after script sent. (920) 788-8888.

25. Pay for ivermectin and give them your mailing address.

The Smith Pharmacy in Wisconsin can ship to any state. There price is reasonable, around $50. You will pay Push Health about $60 for the doctor consultation. The consultation consists of nothing more than communicating with your doctor through messages on Push Health. Typically the doctor will fill your prescription the same day or next day and send it to the pharmacy. They ship for free, but you can pay more for overnight if needed.

Some pharmacies are overcharging. Other pharmacies cannot ship to all states. For that reason, I have instructed you to select Smith Pharmacy in Wisconsin as they are reasonably priced and can ship to any state. When I got my ivermectin through Push Health, the first pharmacy I selected wanted nearly $400 for ivermectin. Obviously, they were price gouging.

I messaged my doctor on Push Health about the exorbitant price and she recommended Western Colorado Compounding Pharmacy located in Grand Junction,

Colorado. (Ph: 970-243-5050) I called them and their price was only $45.00. I received my ivermectin in 2 days.

However, Western Colorado Compounding can only service Colorado, Utah, and Arizona. If you don't live in one of those states, I recommend you select Smith Pharmacy, as they service all states. If you have any trouble with availability or pricing from a pharmacy message your doctor about it so he or she can recommend a different pharmacy and send your script somewhere else. If you have a script at one pharmacy that is too expensive, once you find a good pharmacy, you can call that pharmacy and just ask them to "pull" that prescription from that pharmacy over to theirs.

It is very important that you don't have your ivermectin prescription sent to Walgreens, CVS, Walmart, or any other such local pharmacy. They will either refuse to fill it, or they will lie to you and say they never got the script from the doctor. They lie about receiving it because they don't want to have a confrontation with people who get angry at them for illegally practicing medicine without a license, which is what they are doing when they interfere with what your doctor prescribed for you. If you accidentally selected a local pharmacy, simply call Smith's pharmacy and ask them to pull the script from the local pharmacy. If your doctor sent it to your local pharmacy and they told you that they don't have it, still call Smith's and ask them to pull it from there.

Your doctor may prescribe other medications for you in addition to ivermectin, especially if you currently have Covid. These other meds may be covered by your insurance. You can ask your doctor to send those scripts to your local pharmacy and have your insurance cover them. Alternatively, you can ask Smith Pharmacy if they can accept your insurance for the non-ivermectin meds. It is just ivermectin that has to be handled differently, without insurance coverage.

An Essential Website

Bookmark the following website: **FLCCC.NET**. That is the website for the *Front Line COVID-19 Critical Care Alliance*, a group of concerned doctors fighting on the front lines treating Covid patients day after day. If you don't trust Big Pharma and prefer to get your medical advice from doctors experienced in treating Covid, this is where you want to go for your information. The URL FLCCC.net will redirect you to https://covid19criticalcare.com, which is the same website. There you will read the following message from these doctors:

"The efficacy of ivermectin is supported by results from 64 controlled trials, 32 of them randomized, and 16 of those were double-blinded, the gold standard of research design... the North Indian state of Uttar Pradesh has effectively eradicated Covid from its population of 241 million people after widely distributing ivermectin in their treatment and prevention protocols for Covid-19."

The amount of information on that website is astounding. You could spend days watching videos, reading studies, and learning of their protocol for Covid. On that site, you will find a couple of PDFs that I suggest you print out and have on hand. You are going to want to use those as a guide if you get Covid. These papers tell you exactly what the dosage is that a person should take. However, if you go through Push Health, as I recommend, you will also have a prescription that tells you how much to take. You will also be able to message your doctor and get questions answered later on if you get sick. Here are the links to the treatment protocols on the FLCCC website:

https://covid19criticalcare.com/wp-content/uploads/2020/11/FLCCC-Alliance-I-MASKplus-Protocol-ENGLISH.pdf https://covid19criticalcare.com/wp-content/uploads/2020/12/FLCCC-Protocols-%E2%80%93-A-Guide-to-the-Management-of-COVID-19.pdf

The FLCC.net website also has information on how to get Ivermectin. If for any reason you don't have luck with the method I have suggested, look at their page. This link tells of doctors that will prescribe ivermectin. If you use one from their list, I recommend you pick one that does telemedicine so you can take care of everything from home. Here is the link:

https://covid19criticalcare.com/ivermectin-in-covid-19/how-to-get-ivermectin/

They also have a page of pharmacies that supply ivermectin. Clicking on any of those pharmacies gives you their website and phone number so you can check on their ivermectin prices. That link is:

https://covid19criticalcare.com/pharmacies/

Incidentally, if you come down with the sniffles, or feel short of breath, or have any possible Covid symptoms, go get tested for Covid immediately. Don't wait. While ivermectin works in every stage of the disease, it is most effective if given early. Testing is free and painless. It is not like it used to be, where they would shove a swab up your nose until it feels like it's touching your brain. Now they just lightly swab the inside of your nose and you have an answer in about ten minutes. I have been tested several times. Nothing to it. It's fast, easy, and free. Update: testing materials are not as available as they used to be. If you cannot get tested and you think you might have Covid, you may want to consider starting ivermectin. You can message your doctor on Push Health and have that discussion.

If you test positive, you most likely do have Covid. But if you test negative that's another story. Rapid tests come with a high degree of false negative results. Depending on how far along you are in the illness, and depending upon what brand of test was used, accuracy can vary from 34 to 72 percent.[29] So, testing negative on a rapid test does not mean you don't have Covid. If you test negative but you think you may have Covid, have a discussion with your doctor about further testing.

You will note from the FLCCC.net website that certain over-the-counter supplements are very important. You can get these at your local vitamin/health food store. These are vitamin D3, vitamin C, quercetin, zinc and black seed oil (*nigella sativa*). I recommend you get these on hand before you get sick. These nutrients are important not only if you have Covid, but also as an immune system booster to help with the prevention of any viral illness. I cannot overemphasize the importance of taking the recommended supplements along with the other prescription medications recommended on that website. See the treatment protocols in the links above for the details.

Another recommendation on the alliance website is to use Scope and a nasal spray regularly to help reduce the viral load so that your immune system has less to deal with. Xlear is a nasal spray that has been said to reduce the viral load of Covid. Big Pharma has tried to make problems for the makers of Xlear. The FDA came down on them for saying washing out your nose with Xlear can help with Covid.

What lunacy. I suppose if someone said, "Wash your hands with our soap to help prevent the spread of Covid" then the soap company would be in trouble with the FDA. In an attempt to deal with the meddling bureaucracy of Big Pharma, Xlear applied for an Emergency Use Authorization. In response, the FDA said that since Xlear

---

[29] *https://www.healthline.com/health/how-accurate-are-rapid-covid-tests#how-accurate-is-it*

was apparently effective against Covid, it therefore is a drug and thus cannot be sold over-the-counter.

Did you follow that? Xlear is forbidden to say their over-the-counter product is effective against Covid unless they procure an EUA, and they can't apply for an EUA because, since it is effective against Covid, it is, therefore, a drug and cannot be sold over-the-counter. Only a government bureaucrat could think up such nonsense. Anyway, you can still get Xlear over the counter. You can order it online from Amazon.

Black seed oil is available over-the-counter from health food and vitamin stores. It is particularly interesting. It contains a compound called thymoquinone. The alliance recommends using this if ivermectin cannot be obtained. They also suggest using it along with ivermectin. A clinical study was done on black seed oil, and there is an interesting medical review of that study which can be seen online. Here is a link to that video: https://youtu.be/SOwa6-EOohI

If you have Covid I recommend you send someone right away to get black seed oil. You can buy that immediately at your local vitamin store and begin using it. Amazingly, even the NIH admits it's viability for combatting Covid. They have a position paper on black seed oil. The link is in the footnotes.[30] Here is part of what the NIH says:

Thymoquinone (TQ), the main active ingredient of black seed oil, possesses antioxidant, anti-inflammatory, antiviral, antimicrobial, immunomodulatory and anticoagulant activities. TQ also increases the activity and number of cytokine suppressors, lymphocytes, natural killer cells, and macrophages, and it has demonstrated antiviral potential against a number of viruses, including murine cytomegalovirus, Epstein-Barr virus, hepatitis C virus, human immunodeficiency virus, and other

---

coronaviruses. Recently, TQ has demonstrated notable antiviral activity against a SARSCoV-2 strain isolated from Egyptian patients and, interestingly, molecular docking studies have also shown that TQ could potentially inhibit COVID-19 development through binding to the receptor-binding domain on the spike and envelope proteins of SARS-CoV-2, which may hinder virus entry into the host cell and inhibit its ion channel and pore forming activity. Other studies have shown that TQ may have an inhibitory effect on SARS CoV2 proteases, which could diminish viral replication, and it has also demonstrated good antagonism to angiotensin-converting enzyme 2 receptors, allowing it to interfere with virus uptake into the host cell. Several studies have also noted its potential protective capability against numerous chronic diseases and conditions, including diabetes, hypertension, dyslipidemia, asthma, renal dysfunction and malignancy…Overall, the existing studies highlight the immense potential of TQ as an effective antiviral agent against COVID-19, a premise which is highly supported by the molecular docking studies examining TQ's effects against various virus and host cell targets, which are discussed in more detail in the following section…TQ appears to be a promising therapeutic option for managing COVID-19 and its complications, and clinical trials in COVID-19 patients to examine the beneficial effects of TQ are thus highly recommended.

I am taking black seed oil daily as a potential preventative against Covid, colds and flu and for its wide-ranging health benefits.

Another good product to have on hand to use for prevention is *Taffix*, a product invented in Israel. It is a nose spray that protects from Covid, as well as flu and cold viruses. I use it anytime I am in public. Controlled trials have proven its effectiveness, whereas the efficacy of wearing a cloth obedience mask to stop Covid has never been established by any clinical studies. Here is a website with information about Taffix: https://www.nasuspharma.com/taffix/

You can order Taffix from Ebay.com. That is where I got mine. It comes all the way from Israel so it takes a few weeks.

The Underground Railroad

I recommend using the legal method I described previously – getting a prescription from an online doctor and receiving the medication from an American pharmacy. That is legal, cheap, and then you have a doctor to advise you. However, for entertainment purposes only, perhaps you would like to know what some people are doing to get their ivermectin. It is rather interesting, and not surprising, that Big Pharma's war on ivermectin and hydroxychloroquine has created a sort of underground railroad through which many people are getting their medication another way.

On Facebook, one is not allowed to discuss ivermectin in a positive light. Posts that speak of ivermectin being advantageous against Covid are fact-checked and blocked. The offending account may be taken down. YouTube and Google search results are skewed to hide any videos or websites that speak favorably of hydroxy or ivermectin. They have all conspired together against anyone knowing about these wonderful therapeutics.

To get the truth on some things you have to go to a platform that permits free speech. MeWe.com is one such place. It is an alternative to Facebook. If you set up a free account on MeWe you can do a search for ivermectin groups where the medication is discussed without censorship.

There you will find a world of ivermectin users who have been forced underground. There are groups on MeWe that center around ordering ivermectin from overseas without a prescription. The group discussions cover where to order, the success people have had ordering from various companies, and their own personal experiences with the medicine. The general consensus in the chat groups seems to be that people are receiving their medications after 2 to 4 weeks and that it has been effective for them with no negative side effects.

A website frequently mentioned on those sites is www.AllDayChemist.com On that webpage you simply enter "ivermectin" in the search window at top, make your selection of quantity. This is the human version of the medicine, the same as you get with a prescription. However, this website doesn't require a prescription. The medication is much cheaper here compared to what one would pay at an American pharmacy. You simply click "Add to Cart" and the select "Check Out." You pay with eCheck – you enter your bank routing number and account number. It comes from India so it takes a few weeks to arrive. This information is provided for entertainment purposes only. I recommend Push Health.

There are also discussion groups on MeWe about using ivermectin made for horses. The conspiratorial ban of ivermectin has created a group of people who feel they have no other option than to resort to using veterinary medicines. This is an unwise choice, yet who are we to judge. People will do what they must to save the life of a loved one.

The use of veterinarian medicine has opened the door for fake news outlets to report that ivermectin is nothing but horse de-wormer. As mentioned previously, ivermectin is a medicine used both by doctors and veterinarians. Ivermectin for horses is very cheap and is available without a prescription. It used to be sold at Tractor Supply, but those stores appear to not carry it anymore. However, it is readily available online on eBay, Amazon, and numerous other places.

Calculating the correct dosage when using the veterinarian form requires a bit of math which can be found in these discussion groups. Here is a sample post:

A full tube of ivermectin for horses comes with a measuring apparatus based on the weight of the animal. One entire tube of 6.08 grams would be needed to treat a 1250 lb horse at a 0.2mg/kg dose. To calculate the dosage for humans, realize that 1kg=2.21 pounds. An example calculation: 200 lb / 2.21= 90.5 kg x 0.4 = 36.2 Mg of ivermectin. Don't buy anything that says plus, gold or super as they contain added parasitic chemicals.

As can be seen, using veterinary ivermectin comes with the risk of miscalculating and over or under-dosing. I want to reiterate that these "underground" methods are risky. I went the route of using an American online doctor to get a legal prescription from an American pharmacy. That is the best way. I absolutely do not endorse the use of veterinary ivermectin. I show the above calculations only to illustrate how easy it would be to make an unsafe mistake in dosage.

Dr. Hector Carvallo, a medical doctor in Argentina who is an expert in the treatment of Covid patients with ivermectin cautions against using veterinary ivermectin, saying:

Now, there are veterinary formulations of ivermectin. Do not use these, as they typically contain polyethylene glycol (PEG), which is toxic to humans. Ironically, the COVID shots actually contain PEG. Many are allergic to this substance, which is why anaphylaxis is such a common acute side effect of the jabs.[31]

---

[31] https://deathship.wordpress.com/2021/10/11/argentinian-doctor-shares-his-ivermectin-experience/

I would only advise consulting with a licensed medical practitioner about procuring a legal prescription from an American doctor. Procuring ivermectin for human use by presenting a prescription to a compounding pharmacy is the only legal and safe method to pursue.

I have only shared the information above about veterinary ivermectin to show the conditions that have been created by the revolving-door complicity between the FDA and Big Pharma. This flawed relationship has created an environment susceptible to corruption, which has resulted in people resorting to unsafe methods of procuring medicine. There needs to be new legislation to fix this problem. We need government-financed studies overseen by committees that have no connection to Big Pharma, advisory boards that care about curing disease regardless of profitability. Specifically, we need to finance studies on using repurposed older medications for current illnesses.

Now that you know how to get medicines to protect yourself from Covid let us turn our attention once again to the parameters of the Covid conspiracy. We shall analyze further the coconspirators and their motives while considering the spiritual ramifications of the Covid pandemic in the light of prophetic Scripture.

10

Opening Pandora's Box

The new mRNA vaccines come with significant risk. We don't know what horrific effects might be discovered years from now. Released under an Emergency Use Authorization (EUA), these vaccinations have not received anywhere close to the same amount of safety testing that a normal vaccine gets. Nevertheless, left-wing politicians are attempting to mandate that people be vaccinated against their will. New York City recently imposed a vaccine mandate for all private-sector employers. Anyone living in New York City will lose their job unless they take the jab.

Parents are worried that mandates for children will be next. Across the nation, many have refused vaccination and as a result, countless numbers have lost their jobs. In the face of this resistance, Big Pharma and leftist politicians have attempted to ramp up fear of the virus. They figured out that if you can engender enough fear in people, you can get them to do what you want. Fearmongering has thus become a tactic of the left.

Attorneys Mary Holland and Greg Glaser of the Children's Health Defense want people to know that a government mandate of products authorized under an Emergency Use Authorization (EUA) violates federal law. The law states that if a vaccine has been issued under an EUA it is not fully licensed and must be voluntary. A private party, such as an employer, school, or hospital cannot circumvent the EUA law, which prohibits mandates. Their website is here:

Molnupiravir

The drug companies have now begun work on inventing a pill for early treatment – an expensive one with a new patent. The insane policy of the WHO, FDA, NIH, and CDC of "wait at home until you turn blue" was wearing thin and people were asking questions about ivermectin. Coming out with a pill to take on day one of infection would be advantageous now, just so long as it was really expensive.

One of these new drugs being released is called molnupiravir. Produced by Merck and Ridgeback Biotherapeutics, this new drug has been fast-tracked for use by the FDA with an Emergency Use Authorization. Clinical trials were stopped early to rush the drug to market. It has been approved for use in the UK and the U.S. government has contracted to pay approximately 1.2 billion dollars for 1.7 million courses of the medication.

Molnupiravir is a drug king's dream come true. Cheap to manufacture, Merck stands to make windfall profits. They are selling it for 35 to 40 times more than what it costs to manufacture. U.S. taxpayers are going to be paying $712.00 per course. But there is more to worry about than just the cost.

Without the testing which full FDA approval would require, the long-term effects of this drug will not be known for years to come. Molnupiravir is similar to remdesivir in its mechanism of action and we know that remdesivir can be damaging to the kidneys. Is there a risk for kidney damage to those who take molnupiravir? Are there other dangers? We don't know.

What we do know is this: Molnupiravir is converted in the liver and there is a safety concern that the metabolite action could also be mutagenic, that is, cancerous. There is also concern the drug's action could trigger birth defects in a fetus. While Merck says that's not going to be a problem, Dr. John Campbell, who has studied the drug's action, says evidence he's looking at shows "it at least needs looking into" because "if it stops the normal replication of RNA, is it going to stop the normal replication of our DNA?"[32]

The effectiveness of molnupiravir is not as high as other older medicines. According to data from Merck, molnupiravir reduced hospitalizations or deaths by 50% in 385 participants in the trial, if given early. Whereas studies have shown that ivermectin is 86% effective prophylactically, at least 66% effective in early treatment, and 36% effective in late treatment. Some studies have shown even much higher efficacy for ivermectin when given with zinc and other nutrients. See the footnote for specifics.[33]

Bottom line: Ivermectin is cheaper, safer, and more effective than molnupiravir. It is fully FDA approved and has been around for decades so it has no mysterious effects that we don't know about. But molnupiravir has got one thing that ivermectin does not have – the ability to create massive profits for the maker. Ivermectin is just too inexpensive to do Merck any good, selling for about $30 for a course of the medicine.

All medicines come with some risks. Let's examine the risks associated with some widely used medicines. Here are the stats according to the CDC:

---

[32] https://rubyraymedia.com/index.php/top-stories/us-view-all-articles/magnificent-mercola-comparing-ivermectin-to-merck-s-new-molnupiravir?format=amp

[33] https://covid19criticalcare.com/wp-content/uploads/2020/11/FLCCC-Alliance-I-MASKplus-Protocol-ENGLISH.pdf

Acetaminophen – 458 deaths <u>per year</u>[34]

Aspirin – 3,000 deaths <u>per year.</u>[35]

Ibuprofen – 16,000 deaths <u>per year</u>[36]

Covid Vaccines – 16,766 deaths <u>in the past year.</u>[37]

How does that compare with ivermectin, which has been prescribed billions of times? Here is what the CDC says the deaths are from ivermectin for the entire past 25 years:

Ivermectin – 379 deaths worldwide <u>over 25 years</u>

There you have it. ivermectin is far safer than acetaminophen, aspirin, ibuprofen, or the Covid vaccine. I bet you won't hear that interesting bit of information on the evening news. Rather quite the opposite. There have been multitudes of news stories deriding ivermectin as "horse medicine" or "horse de-wormer" and dangerous for humans. Even the FDA, ever carrying the water for Big Pharma, jumped in with an ad full of dire warnings of dangerous side effects, saying: *You are not a horse. You are not a cow. Seriously, y'all. Stop it.*

You will notice on the list of deaths per year on the previous page that I do not mention molnupiravir. That is because there is no data on this brand-new drug. We won't know for a few years how dangerous it is. Dr. William A. Haseltine has stated that if molnupiravir is approved for

<hr>

[34] *https://pubmed.ncbi.nlm.nih.gov/16294364/*

[35] *https://www.huffingtonpost.co.uk/entry/daily-aspirin-causes-more-than-3000-deaths-per-year-scientists-warn_uk_593fb481e4b0b13f2c6daa10*

[36] *https://www.institutefornaturalhealing.com/2017/05/just-one-day-on-ibuprofen-increases-your-chance-of-a-heart-attack/*

[37] *https://www.christianitydaily.com/articles/13646/20211018/senator-says-covid-vaccine-mandates-are-pointless-following-thousands-of-deaths-injuries-after-the-jabs.htm*

use, which it already has, then "we are potentially headed towards a world-class disaster."[38]

I shall explain, in condensed form what Dr. Haseltine says. First, let me tell you who the good doctor is. Doctor Haseltine is a former Harvard professor who founded and chaired Harvard's Division of Biochemical Pharmacology that has studied mutagenesis and the long-term effects of damaged DNA. Dr. Haseltine has educated a generation of doctors at Harvard Medical School, designed the strategy to develop the first treatment for HIV/AIDS, is well known for his groundbreaking work on cancer, and led the team that pioneered the development of new drugs based on information from the human genome.

While Dr. Haseltine says there most certainly is a risk of cancer and birth defects for those who take molnupiravir, he explains there is an even greater danger: Molnupiravir's modus operandi is to function as a *mutagenic nucleotide analogue* which introduces errors in the SARS-COV-2 RNA at the time of replication.[39] What's so bad about that? I shall explain.

Molnupiravir makes the virus have genetic mutations when replicating, with the idea of those mutations being so severe as to stop the replication. But what if some mutations don't stop the replication and end up creating a new host of variants of the virus? What if those variants are more contagious or more deadly, or both? This is what Dr. Haseltine is worried about. Now you understand why Dr. Haseltine says *"we are potentially headed towards a world-class disaster."*

---

[38] *https://www.forbes.com/sites/williamhaseltine/2021/11/01/supercharging-new-viral-variants-the-dangers-of-molnupiravir-part-1/?sh=1f44166a6b15*

[39] *https://trialsitenews.com/is-molnupiravir-a-global-catastrophic-threat*

And all this risk is so completely unnecessary. Hydroxy and ivermectin are existing drugs that have full FDA approval and have been safely used for many years. Yet, in the pursuit of massive profits by these multinational drug companies, Pandora's box is being opened. What horrors escape from there into the world, once released, may never again be contained.

The dangers of these experimental drugs may release a plague of biblical proportions that dwarfs what we have already experienced. While Dr. Haseltine admits there are legitimate concerns about cancer, he goes on to say that molnupiravir presents, *"a danger that is far greater and potentially far deadlier: the drug's potential to supercharge SARS-CoV-2 mutations and unleash a more virulent variant upon the world."* Dr. Haseltine has given warning. Is anyone listening? What horrors are the drug companies releasing from Pandora's box? It would seem that Dr. Fauci-Stein is not the only mad scientist on the loose.

11

Globalism

In this chapter, I will bring to light the spiritual dimension behind the pandemic and possible reasons for the inexplicably reckless actions of multinational pharmaceutical corporations. I intend to get political and religious as I give a Christian perspective on current events. If you have no interest in that, feel free to skip the following chapters. I understand it is not everyone's cup of tea. On the other hand, if you are curious as to the master plan behind the Covid chaos, this chapter is for you.

Why are some of these companies operating with such disregard for possible consequences? Why are they ignoring existing medicines? Is it all just because of greed, or is there something else at play? Is there a worldwide master plan of sinister intent? What is coming next? This chapter will examine these questions.

In chapter three I touched upon the global interests of transnational corporations that have disregard for the national interests of the people of their own country. This brings us to the subject of globalism. If you were to ask a globalist what globalism actually is, you might hear something like this:

"Globalism is the future! Nationalism causes wars and trade imbalance. We need to all come together and work for the common good of the world and not just the self-interest of a particular nation. The Globalist New World Order is the next step in man's evolution to a better life!"

Sounds great, doesn't it? Not if you're a Christian and know a little bit about end-time Bible prophecy. Truth be told, the glittering promise of a new globalist age that is all roses is nothing but smoke and mirrors. Whenever someone promises a perfect utopia our internal deception detector should go off. Those who promote globalism, a new world order, or one-world anything, are people who do not have a Christian worldview. Christians realize that any method for fixing this broken world that intentionally leaves out the Bible, devotion to God, love of our fellow man, and Jesus Christ, is a solution that is doomed to failure. God has declared:

"For my thoughts are not your thoughts, neither are your ways my ways, declares the Lord. For as the heavens are higher than the earth, so are my ways higher than your ways and my thoughts than your thoughts." (Isaiah 55:8-9)

Man's First Attempt at Globalism

Globalism is a concept invented by man. It is interesting to note that it is not a new invention, but an old one. In Genesis Chapter 11 we read that after the flood of Noah, *"the whole world had one language and a common speech."* The people united together in an ambitious one-world plan. Even though God had instructed them to scatter across the world and inhabit it, they chose to disobey. They wanted to stay in one place and have a one-world government.

Out of pride, the people began construction of the infamous Tower of Babel that they believed would demonstrate their transcendent unified power and ability. Although mankind was interested in what they could accomplish together, God saw things differently. He knew that if mankind unified, man's fallen spiritual state would result in their science and technology advancing faster than their wisdom. As a consequence, their global unity would be their undoing.

God was more interested in mankind obeying their Creator and learning to love others than He was in seeing them achieve great accomplishments of architecture and science. While man often sees technology as a savior, God knows that only following His will can truly bring salvation. God was not pleased with the disobedience and pride displayed at Babel. Holy Scripture tells us that God's response was to break the people up into groups by scrambling their language.

Instantly, people were speaking many different languages. Work on their great tower and their city came to a halt. They scattered to the four winds, everyone gathering together with people they could understand. This is what gave rise to all the various nations and races of people. From this historical event, we learn that God's plan for the world is nationalism, not one-world government or globalism.

Satan's Final Attempt at Globalism

Since that time, Satan has often tempted man to come together into a one-world government. Many attempts at global conquest have been attempted, the most notable being that of Adolf Hitler. In recent times, the same thing is being attempted through globalization. Bible prophecy predicts that in the last days, Satan's Antichrist will finally accomplish this, but only for a short time. Then God will put an end to it.

Daniel chapters 2 and 9, 2 Thessalonians 2:1-12, and Revelation chapter 17 instruct us that out of Europe and part of Asia – from the general geographical area that was once part of the old Roman Empire – will arise a world leader of unspeakable evil, known as the Antichrist. He will gain control over a ten-nation confederacy of that region. That confederacy will attempt, unsuccessfully, to erase national lines by melding the people together. Scripture says, *"In that you saw the iron mixed with common clay, they will combine with one another in their descendants; but they will not adhere to one another, just as iron does not combine with pottery."* (Daniel 2:43)

Nevertheless, for a time the Antichrist will achieve a one-world government, in defiance of God's decree of nationalism. Scripture says of the Antichrist: *"And power was given him over all kindreds, and tongues, and nations; over every tribe, and people, and tongue, and nation."* (Revelation 13:7) A globalist one-world government is the devil's plan, not God's.

The Virtue of Nationalism

Nationalism is a polity of independent nations with a political order based on the nation-state seeking the freedom of self-determination and self-rule. The nations of the world were created by God himself at the tower of Babel when he supernaturally intervened by giving multitudes of languages. God's word says:

"From one man he made all the nations, that they should inhabit the whole earth; and he marked out their appointed times in history and the boundaries of their lands." (Acts 17:6)

So you see, God's word says that the Lord made the nations and that their borders were appointed by Him. Thus, the erasure or disregard of a national border is contrary to His will. Jesus said, *"What therefore God hath joined together, let not man put asunder."* Jesus was speaking of marriage in that context, but the principle applies to whatever God has joined together, whether it be a husband and wife, a baby in the womb, or contiguous national borders.

Nationalism is a virtue, it being God's ordained plan since the tower of Babel. God often speaks of his plans for specific nations. For example, In Genesis 12:2 God promises to Abraham, *"And I will make of thee a great nation, and I will bless thee."* Again, speaking of Abraham, God says he does this so that *'all the nations of the earth shall be blessed in him"* (Gen 18:18). God does not see the world as one, but as a conglomerate of nations. That was and is His intention for mankind. If it was not, He would have told us. The nationalism offered unto Israel and all other nations of the earth is a counter-narrative to the globalism of Babel. All through scripture we find God declaring that it is His will which is the true progenitor of nations. It is God who gave us nations with borders. Now you understand why the god-hating, baby-killing, Bible-bashing left hates borders – it is because borders are of God.

God has instituted a proper priority in all things. God has intended that people have their primary responsibility to their own family first, then to others of their country, and then to other nations. A man who would feed a child in Africa while letting his own wife and child starve has his priorities all mixed up. Patriotism to one's own nation has a precedent, and so long as that country follows the will of God, so its people should support it. One's primary responsibility is owed first to one's own country. If that country goes astray, then true patriotism means doing all possible to help set that country back upon a correct path. Bottom line: If God considers nations and borders a good work of His doing, then we should oppose them being minimized and denigrated.

The Evils of Globalism

Satan, who hates all that God does, has attempted to fight against God's plan of nationalism with globalism and this has resulted in untold evil. While the siren-song of globalism promises to care for the less fortunate countries of the world, it is actually the opposite. Globalism is the mass exploitation of cheap labor, and in some instances, slave labor.

It is the expansion of corporatocracy without concern for the environment, while virtue signaling with meaningless tripe about climate change. It is the sacrifice of one's own nation upon the altar of greed and corruption. It is rebellion against one's own national authority in a power-mad quest by a select elite – international financiers, central bankers, transnational corporations, and politicians – to control the world.

Carroll Quigley (1910-1977) was a highly respected professor at Georgetown University, Princeton, and Harvard and a consultant to the U.S. Department of Defense. He explained that globalism has…

the far-reaching aim, nothing less than to create a world system of financial control in private hands able to dominate the political system of each country and the economy of the world as a whole. This system was to be controlled...to manipulate foreign exchanges, to influence the level of economic activity in the country, and to influence cooperative politicians by subsequent economic rewards in the business world." – Carroll Quigley, Tragedy and Hope[40]

Brandon Smith, a well-known investigative journalist, has a succinct definition of globalism:

"The people behind the effort to enforce globalism are tied together by a particular ideology, perhaps even a cult-like religion, in which they envision a world order as described in Plato's Republic. They believe that they are "chosen" either by fate, destiny, or genetics to rule as philosopher kings over the rest of us. They believe that they are the wisest and most capable that humanity has to offer, and that

---

[40] http://www.amzn.com/094500110X

through evolutionary means, they can create chaos and order out of thin air and mold society at will."[41]

Henry Kissinger, former Secretary of State and National Security Advisor under President Nixon was an avowed globalist. He emphasized the importance of the United States jumping on the globalist band wagon:

"The New World Order cannot happen without U.S. participation, as we are the single most significant component. Yes, there will be a New World Order, and it will force the United States to change its perceptions." – Henry Kissinger, World Action Council, April 19, 1994

Journalist Brandon Smith says it well:

"While some people see globalism as a 'natural offshoot' of free markets or the inevitable outcome of economic progress, the reality is that the simplest explanation (given the evidence at hand) is that globalism is an outright war waged against the ideal of sovereign peoples and nations. It is a guerrilla war, or fourth generation warfare, waged by a small group of elites against the rest of us."

To that wisdom, I simply say: Globalism is dominant colonialism on steroids. God gave us nations with borders. We dismantle them at our own peril.

Agendas

I said all that to say this: There is a master agenda to all that has happened since 2020. The coronavirus that escaped from the bio-weapons lab in Wuhan was manmade, but its inspiration was demonically belched forth from the bowels of Hell with Satan as its chief architect. The pandemic made it possible for the Democratic Party in America to illegally circumvent election law in battleground states, thus

---

allowing unprecedented mail-in voting that was ripe with fraud. Proven fact.[42] President Trump's landslide victory was stolen and turned into a narrow win for Joe Biden. Established truth.[43]

What has been the consequence of the installation of a weak and corrupt old man with cognitive difficulties into the highest office of a world superpower? The past year has shown that he is easily controlled by the most radical elements of his party. Unscrupulous politicians seduced by globalism have convinced Biden to dismantle the southern border of the United States.

In the past year, over one million illegal aliens (update: It is now ten million) have trespassed through our southern border from over 165 countries around the world. And that is just the ones that have been documented. Perhaps twice that number from who-knows-where coming to do who-knows-what have disappeared into the night, unapprehended. The motive of liberals in promoting this border invasion is to obtain new voters for the Democratic Party so that they can stay in power indefinitely. But the motive of the demonic forces behind this is far more sinister. It is part of a concerted plan to bring down the United States.

The children now in control of the government are busy chasing their tail with the global-warming fairytale. When they are not crying that the sky is falling, they are busy amusing themselves playing house with socialism and gender-mania. In the meantime, oil pipelines are being shut down, massive and foolish spending is feeding inflation, and the forced firing of unprecedented numbers of the unvaccinated has put the country on the verge of dangerous

---

[42] *For the evidence of the stolen election go to* *https://frankspeech.com*

[43] *https://cdn.michaeljlindell.com/downloads/fix2020first/states-v-us-and-states-compl-2021-11-23.pdf*

shortages of essential goods and services throughout the country. Why this dangerous foolishness? Because Satan has an agenda that requires the humiliation and subjugation of America. I repeat the words of Henry Kissinger:

"The New World Order cannot happen without U.S. participation, as we are the single most significant component."

Washington D.C. is infected with powerful politicians who have a demonically inspired hatred for America as it was founded. That is why they brazenly say, as was done under the Obama-Biden regime, that they intend to "fundamentally change America." America must go down. Its Christian roots must be rooted out and burned. Nationalism must go out the window. What is best for the American people must be denigrated. "Make America Great Again" must be reinterpreted to somehow mean white supremacy. That slogan is hated because it is the antithesis of globalism. Individual rights must be subjugated to the power of the state so that America may coalesce and align with the new world order.

That is the demonic agenda behind current events. While the United States writhes in the turmoil of its self-inflicted demise, bad actors across the world sense their opportunity. With a president that has accepted bribes from Russia and China running America, foreign powers know they have nothing to fear from a man that can be bought. China has taken Hong Kong and is licking its chops over Taiwan. North Korea is once again moving full steam ahead on its nuclear weapons and ballistic missile programs and is once again flying ballistic missiles over the Sea of Japan. Islamic terrorists now have Afghanistan as a base to attack from, along with 85 billion dollars' worth of military equipment that Biden left for them to use. As I write this, thousands of abandoned American citizens left behind in Afghanistan, are being hunted by the Taliban and war is raging in Ukraine.

Suddenly the dogs of war are running loose and one wonders, who let the dogs out? Amazing that one stolen election in the United States could do so much damage to the world. The bottom line is this. We are living in the last days foretold in the ancient scriptures of the Bible. Satan is setting the stage for the Antichrist and his one-world government. That involves getting the United States out of the way by transforming it into something unrecognizable. Resistance to totalitarianism and globalism must be quashed. Making people afraid is a tool in that process. Fearful people are easier to control. Those who are panicked will put up with the loss of their freedoms much more readily.

Satan's agenda involves a great shaking and realignment of power around the globe. We are seeing it happen before our very eyes. When we have eyes to see, we understand why politicians want everyone to wear an "obedience mask."[44] It helps engender more fear, which triggers more obedience. Every night on Fox News, Newsmax, One America News, and FrankSpeech.com, newscasters chronicle the madness of recent actions ordered from the White House. They scratch their heads at the insanity and ask rhetorically, "Why are they doing this." Now you know.

As a Christian, I know my real citizenship is in heaven, from where we await a Savior, the Lord Jesus Christ who will soon return and catch us away to that heavenly home he has prepared for us. Each of us can turn to God in prayer, seeking inner tranquility and supernatural wisdom that guides us safely through trouble. I pray that God grants a reprieve for America, that a revival will turn the heart of the nation back to Him, that we may have more time to tell others of the forgiveness and new life to be found in Christ.

---

[44] *There are no scientific studies that show a cloth mask is effective against Covid. The disease is rampant in states that have strict mask mandates. This shows how ineffective they are. But they are effective at making people both obedient and afraid.*

Whether or not the end of days is upon us, or if there is yet more time, I do not know. The return of Christ to rescue His Church is imminent. Perhaps He will come tomorrow. But this one thing I have determined, if our beloved country is to go down in ashes, if baby-killing God-haters are going to take over and if the foundation of America shall fall, I have determined this one thing: As far as I am concerned, it will not go down without a fight. When the Lord returns may He find us busy saving souls, speaking truth to power, and seeking healing for our country.

Practical Steps

It is a day for the Church to awaken and call our nation to repentance. It is time for Christians to be vocal about sin, righteousness, and the judgment to come. We all must be politically involved and make our voice heard. Plato said, *"The price of apathy towards public affairs is to be ruled by evil men."* For the sake of our children and grandchildren, we must fight to save this great nation. The pen is mightier than the sword and I intend to warn all that will listen. Across the nation men and women of decent character are standing up and shouting, "Enough already!" Let us join together and save our country.

Where do we start? We can start by protecting ourselves and our families against death by the virus unleashed by the Chinese Communist Party. The next chapter will tell you how. For winning back America, get involved politically and oppose the destructive actions of the Democratic Party, and the RINOs[45] in the Republican Party. Work with your church on being more evangelical in bringing Christ to your community. It is a time for boldness.

Eighteen states have passed election reform laws this year. Make certain that your state is working to fix our

---

[45] *RINO: Republican In Name Only*

broken and vulnerable election system so that we will never have another stolen election. Search Google for "election reform *state*" where "*state*" is replaced by the state where you live. Look for an organization that is working on that and join them. If Google gives you no results, then use the search engine https://www.4conservative.com. Google skews search results so that conservatives cannot find the information they need.

Write to your representatives and ask how you can help. Get involved in your local school and make sure that your children are not being indoctrinated with Marxism, critical race theory, homosexual behavior, climate change theory, and evolution. Asking questions at a school board meeting may get you marked by the FBI as a domestic terrorist but so be it.[46] We must not let intimidation from the left stop us. The following websites will get you started in helping to save our nation.

https://conventionofstates.com

https://ifapray.org/about/

https://frankspeech.com

---

[46] *https://tfiglobalnews.com/2021/11/13/outspoken-parents-will-be-categorized-as-domestic-terrorists-in-bidens-usa/*

12

The Covid Conspiracy

Hermann Göring, convicted war criminal and high-ranking Nazi official under Adolf Hitler, while languishing in a cell at the Nuremberg trials, had this to say about how they got the German people to follow them to destruction:

It is always a simple matter to drag the people along whether it is a democracy, a fascist dictatorship, or a parliament, or a communist dictatorship. Voice or no voice, the people can always be brought to the bidding of the leaders. That is easy. All you have to do is tell them they are being attacked, and denounce the pacifists for lack of patriotism, and exposing the country to greater danger. It works the same in any country.[47]

Göring admitted that the Nazi party used fear to *"drag the people along"* and get them to *"do the bidding of the leaders."* He explains how it is done: *"All you have to do is tell them they are being attacked..."*

That is exactly what is happening in America. The conspirators of the pandemic are saying, "We are being attacked by a virus, but more than that we are being attacked by people that don't obey us!" Biden recently said, *"Look, the only pandemic we have is among the*

---

unvaccinated." With an angry countenance, he scolded the American people, saying, *"Our patience is wearing thin!"* Now we have forcible vaccinations being done to people against their will. We have lockdowns, church and business closures, mask mandates, and the curtailing of the 1st Amendment. People critical of the government are being arrested. The population accepts it. Why? Because they are afraid. Now hear the words of the despot one more time:

"All you have to do is tell them they are being attacked, and denounce the pacifists for lack of patriotism, and exposing the country to greater danger. It works the same in any country."

This chapter will examine more fully the spiritual dimensions of the pandemic and how it ties in with biblical end-time prophesy. For additional information on eschatology that goes beyond the scope of this writing, I recommend my book, *End of Days: What the Bible Says Happens Next*, available on Amazon. See the link in the footnote.[48] For more information on the political landscape of America, I recommend my book, *Hidden History: The Untold Story of the Democratic Party*.[49]

The Covid Conspiracy is multifaceted, involving collusion between six groups of coconspirators.

Let us now review who these players are and their motives. Here is the list:

1. Satan, the Antichrist, and The Harlot of Revelation 17
2. Big Pharma – Federal (Regulatory Agencies)
3. Big Pharma – Corporate (Multinational Corporations)
4. Big Tech – Facebook, Google, YouTube, and Twitter
5. Fake News Media – CNN, CBS, NBC, ABC, and MSNBC

---

[48] *https://www.amzn.com/B08HPN4LTV*

[49] *www.amzn.com/B08VR7WR1N*

6. The Democratic Party

We will now consider and analyze the role and motives of each of the conspirators.

Satan

Satan is using the pandemic to increase totalitarianism in the world and decrease the ability and will of America to hold back the forces of darkness being expressed as aggressive territorial expansionism by certain foreign powers. China, Russia, and North Korea are rattling their sabers as they sense weakness and lack of resolve from the Biden regime. The pandemic made it possible for the Democratic Party to steal the 2020 Presidential election with massive mail-in voter fraud[50] and install the Biden regime in the White House, giving rise to the current international instability.

Since time immemorial the devil has been desirous to place a man in charge of the world to be his Antichrist. History is littered with failed attempts at this. Genghis Khan, Alexander the Great, Julius Caesar, Napoleon Bonaparte, and Adolf Hitler to name a few. The ancient prophecies of the Bible predict that in the last days the devil will be successful at finally achieving a global empire with the Antichrist ruling.

Scripture tells us that *"the secret power of lawlessness"* (2 Thessalonians 2:7) is already at work and will increase in the last days to make way for the Antichrist. I believe that is what we are seeing now. The Apostle Paul warned us of what is happening in America today:

---

[50] *One example: The recent Arizona audit revealing massive fraud shows what took place in battleground states. The audit showed "57,734 ballots with serious issues…these issues include improper voter registration, improper votes, and discrepancies in the registration." This means Trump won Arizona by almost 50,000 votes. See: https://richardsonpost.com/harryrichardson/23642/maricopa-county-audit-trump-won/*

"But mark this: There will be terrible times in the last days. People will be lovers of themselves, lovers of money, boastful, proud, abusive, disobedient to their parents, ungrateful, unholy, without love, unforgiving, slanderous, without self-control, brutal, not lovers of the good, treacherous, rash, conceited, lovers of pleasure rather than lovers of God— having a form of godliness but denying its power." (2 Timothy 3:1-5)

One need only turn on the evening news to behold riots in the streets of America. In California, liberal Democrats have essentially legalized shoplifting, resulting in widespread theft of merchandise from stores.[51] In Chicago, it is common to have a hundred people shot every weekend.[52] Liberals have so laxened the criminal justice system that dangerous repeat offenders are allowed to roam the streets. In Wisconsin, this liberal foolishness had tragic consequences. A repeat offender, a felon with a long rap sheet of violent crimes, mowed down people with his car, killing six and injuring sixty-two others.[53]

Across the nation, homosexual activists disrupt church services and terrorize Christians.[54] Liberal Democrat governors enforced strict closure rules for churches during the pandemic while allowing strip clubs, liquor stores, and marijuana dispensaries to remain open. According to Outreach Magazine, one in five churches will close forever as a result.[55] The push of the Democratic Party to defund police, empty the prisons, and encourage violent riots has resulted in nationwide chaos.[56] The laws of man are

---

[51] *https://www.hoover.org/research/why-shoplifting-now-de-facto-legal-california*
[52] *https://policetribune.com/chicago-weekend-death-toll-climbs-102-shot-14-killed-including-toddler/*
[53] *https://www.dailymail.co.uk/news/article-10237227/Tucker-Carlson-says-liberal-media-NOT-probe-motives-Waukesha-parade-massacre.html*
[54] *https://www.orthodoxytoday.org/blog/2008/11/homosexual-activists-disrupt-church-service-bash-christians/*
[55] *https://outreachmagazine.com/resources/research-and-trends/59661-research-1-in-5-churches-may-close-due-to-pandemic.html*
[56] *Democrat Representative Rashida Tlaib endorsed a bill last year that would abolish federal prisons over the course of 10 years. See:*

flaunted and the laws of God are utterly disregarded. Yet, the Scripture passage above says that these lawless ones have *"a form of godliness."* Amazingly, these lawless people will have a religion. What does that religion look like? The Bible describes it.

https://dennismichaellynch.com/watch-squad-rep-tlaib-defends-bill-that-would-empty-federal-prisons-in-shocking-interview/

The Harlot Who Rides the Beast

Revelation Chapter 17 foretells an end-time, one-world "harlot" religion that is in collusion with "the beast," that is, the Antichrist. In the Old Testament God often referred to God's people (Israel) as a harlot because of their idolatrous infidelity to God. Since the book of Revelation defines this end-time religion as a harlot, we can anticipate that this false religion will, at least in part, be comprised of apostate Christianity. This religion has, for a time, a symbiotic relationship with the Antichrist. Together they hate born-again biblical Christianity.[57] But the Antichrist also hates the harlot religion, probably because of its Christian roots. Eventually, the Antichrist turns on the woman and destroys her.[58]

This religion is in its infant stages now. It will not reach its final and full manifestation until the final seven years of the age, a time known as The Great Tribulation. Nevertheless, we can see this religion forming today. Part of that manifestation is apparent in the enthusiastic embrace of environmentalism, homosexuality, and abortion by many liberal mainline denominations.[59]

At a service at one such denomination, I recently heard a congregational prayer, not for the salvation of souls, or that America would turn back to God, but that the fish in the sea would have enough food. Last I checked, my Bible says that our Heavenly Father feeds the birds of the air and clothes the flowers of the field.[60] I'm pretty sure he has the fish covered as well. We probably needn't be overly concerned whether the fish have enough other fish to eat.

This change in emphasis of a segment of the Church from saving the souls of men to saving planet Earth is likely reflective of the embryonic stage of the coming one-world

---

[57] *Revelation 17:6*
[58] *Revelation 17:16*
[59] *There are a few Christians within these denominations. That changes at the Rapture.*
[60] *Matthew 6:26-30*

religion, which flouts the laws of God on sexuality and infanticide while claiming religious superiority by virtue of its concern for Mother Earth. This arising "form of religion" sees the world as a sort of divine being that must not be sinned against, rather than what it is: an inanimate object created by God for the benefit and use of man.

The fervent embrace of homosexuality and abortion while failing to call people to a life changed by the power of God is precisely the biblical description of the coming world religion wherein people are *"lovers of pleasure rather than lovers of God— having a form of godliness but denying its power."* Their worried cry that overpopulation is harming Mother Earth gives justification to their sacrament: The sacrifice of unborn children upon their sacred altars of convenience and environmentalism.

While the Christian worldview has always been to consider the Earth an inert object created by God for mankind's habitation, many leftists have adopted a new-age view of the earth, seeing it as though it were a living organism with a soul. This is similar to the ancient neopagan religion known as pantheism, the belief that nature is god. The new earth-worship pantheists are more sophisticated than those of the ancient past with many adherents only ascribing to the pseudo-scientific side of the religion, known as climate change.[61] If a liberal climate change believer thinks that anything is a sin, then the greatest sin of all, in their minds, is the use of fossil fuels.

A Christian worldview understands that God is in control of the Earth and its destiny, that He created the oil in the ground, and He established our weather cycles. A Christian understands that God created the earth to last as long as He intended. Climate change evangelists, if they believe in God at all, think that all this caught God off guard

---

[61] *For a physicist's refutation of global warming alarmism I recommend the book Hot Talk Cold Science, written by four eminent scientists. It is available on Amazon.*

– that the Creator of the universe was completely surprised by global warming and just didn't see it coming. Apparently, they imagine that God just never thought that mankind would burn the oil in the ground to create power and improve their lives

Climate change has been taken up as a major focus by several mainline denominations as well as the Catholic Church. Typically, churches involved in the ecumenical movement are also evangelists for climate change hysteria. Why? Denial of a personal relationship with the Savior leaves one with an emptiness desirous of being filled. These pantheistic Christians of the new age attempt to fill this void with a religion of works, vainly grasping for sanctification through endless evangelism of their global warming gospel.

Increasingly, born-again Christians are the target of their ire for rejecting their unscriptural message. One need only google "Christian climate change deniers" to see a plethora of articles lambasting fundamentalist Christians as being responsible for the destruction of the earth because they don't care about climate change the way they should.[62]

What has all this to do with Covid? The climate change religionists are blaming the Covid pandemic upon climate change. Google "pandemic climate change" and you will see what I mean. Here is a sample of their logic:

"As the planet heats up, animals big and small, on land and in the sea, are headed to the poles to get out of the heat…that means animals are coming into contact with other animals they normally wouldn't, and that creates an opportunity for pathogens to get into new hosts."

Dr. Anthony Fauci agrees, saying *"We have entered a pandemic era."* Never mind that the virus didn't come to us directly from an animal but was a man-modified bat

---

[62] *Here is a sample: https://journals.sagepub.com/doi/full/10.1177/0096340215599789*

virus arising from gain-of-function research funded by Dr. Fauci and accidentally released from the bio-warfare lab in communist China. But please, pay no attention to that man behind the curtain.

So, in the minds of some liberals, born-again Christians are to blame for climate change, which caused the pandemic, which killed millions of people.[63] Thus according to some, Bible-believing fundamentalist Christians are guilty of the death of millions. What recourse will this new religion take against Christians? Here we have another harbinger of the end-time religion that in the future will be described as being *"drunk with the blood of the saints."* (Revelation 17:6)

The Antichrist

The pandemic has caused a paradigm shift in the world on many levels. There has been a fundamental change in the fabric of America. Unless reversed, free elections and constitutional rights are increasingly a thing of the past. Lawlessness is tolerated while government overreach is the norm. The recent trial of Kyle Rittenhouse is an example. A young man who exercised his legal right of self-defense was charged with no legal basis to do so. Although he was exonerated by the jury, mobs of dissidents were permitted to scream profanity and threats within hearing of the jury while they deliberated. Death threats were sent to the judge and the attorneys. They threatened to burn down the town if there was not a guilty verdict.

These thugs have been incited and encouraged by the liberal news media and the Democratic Party. Together they have behaved like a lynch mob out for blood. This is the same Democratic Party that officially kicked God out

---

[63] *I don't mean to imply all people who believe in climate change think this way. Although a large number do, I only refer to some.*

of their party, that is in favor of abortion, transgenderism, and homosexual "marriage."

What is my point? Simply that we are now in a time of lawlessness such as never before, and the party that hates the laws of God is at the forefront. This lawlessness was predicted in Bible prophecy to be a precursor to the coming Antichrist. In short, the pandemic is the tenderizer to soften up the world's attitude towards, and acceptance of, lawless totalitarian barbarism, paving the way for the Antichrist.

Big Pharma

The regulatory agencies of Big Pharma are the FDA, AMA, CDC, NIH, and the WHO. The bureaucracy of these agencies is in cahoots with multinational drug companies such as Moderna, Johnson & Johnson, Pfizer, and others. No doubt there are some fine and decent people who work in high-level positions at these companies. Unfortunately, it only takes one bad apple to spoil the bunch.

The problem is the revolving door between the government regulatory agencies and the drug companies which is conducive to corruption. For example, Scott Gottlieb, former head of the FDA is now on the board of Pfizer. Stephen Hahn, who led the FDA when it authorized Moderna's COVID shots, is now an executive with Flagship Pioneering, the company that launched Moderna. Mark McClellan is a former FDA commissioner. He sits on the board of directors of Johnson & Johnson.[64] As investigative journalist Jordan Schachtel put it:

"Have an experimental drug that needs rapid authorization from the FDA in order to be sold to the masses? Looking to siphon billions of dollars from the U.S. taxpayer for your newfound pharmaceutical product? In today's America,

---

[64] *https://nexusnewsfeed.com/article/geopolitics/revolving-doors-of-fda-and-big-pharma/*

you can buy yourself a former FDA commissioner, and use the public-sector private-sector revolving door system of corruption to impose your will on the American public, and make a windfall for your executives and shareholders in the process. "[65]

The role of Big Pharma in the pandemic is to make as much money as possible. That means keeping the pandemic going as long as possible by forbidding cheap and effective medicines and promoting expensive ones that don't work as well. A secondary role of Big Pharma is to provide the government with whatever information they need to restrict freedom and mandate that these drugs be purchased and injected into unwilling "customers." Getting people accustomed to totalitarian control is the devil's goal in all this. How much of this is intentional and how much is incidental is debatable, but most certainly Satan is pleased with the end result manifested from the selfish actions of his unwitting pawns.

Big Tech

Big Tech consists of Facebook, YouTube, Google, and Twitter. These are monopolies, who together with the fake news media, endeavor to advance the political agenda of the Democratic Party. The owners of these companies are interested in more than money. They want power, and they have it. They influence elections and buy influence in the halls of Congress. Big Tech works to inhibit free speech by restricting and filtering information to the American people so that only a message in harmony with that of the platform of the Democratic Party is presented.

According to an article on the Breitbart News Network, Facebook founder Mark Zuckerberg donated $400 million to orchestrate a "masterpiece of electoral larceny involving

---

[65] *Ibid*

Big Tech oligarchs, activists, and government officials who prioritize partisanship over patriotism."[66] Such massive funding allowed for the circumvention of election laws in order to facilitate voter fraud in favor of the Democratic Party in the 2020 presidential election. The article states:

The 2020 election was stolen because leftists were able to exploit the coronavirus pandemic to weaken, alter, and eliminate laws that were put in place over the course of decades to preserve the integrity of the ballot box. But just as importantly, it was stolen because those same leftists had a thoroughly-crafted plan, and because they were rigorous in its implementation and ruthless in its execution.[67]

There is a pattern to see be seen with Big Tech and Big Pharma monopolies. Once a corporation has all the money it could ever need, it then covets political power, which it then uses to change laws to give itself even more money and power.

Fake News Media

CNN, CBS, NBC, ABC, MSNBC constitute what has become known as the "fake news media," whose reporting is nearly always in line with the message of the Democratic Party, even if that involves bald-faced lies. Juxtaposed against this propaganda arm of the left is the real news media, consisting of NewsMax, One America News (OAN), FrankSpeech.com, and, to a lesser extent, Fox News.

Harvard released a study that analyzed The Wall Street Journal, the New York Times, and The Washington Post, as well as CBS, CNN, FOX, and NBC during the first one hundred days of Trump's presidency. The report revealed

---

[66] *https://www.educationviews.org/robber-baron-zuckerbergs-role-in-influencing-the-election/*

[67] *Ibid*

that CBS coverage was 91% negative and 9% positive. New York Times was 87% negative and 17% positive. Wall Street Journal was 70% neg and 30% positive.[68]

CNN reporter Amber Lyon has revealed that her bosses at CNN attempted to coerce her into bending the truth and fabricating lies. She describes learning first hand that our own government routinely pays CNN to selectively report on certain events and make up fake news stories.[69] The bias of the leftist news media is so well documented that anyone who doesn't recognize it is blinded by a severe case of pollyannaish naiveté.

The Democratic Party

From its inception by Andrew Jackson and Martin Van Buren in 1828, the Democratic Party has been on the side of evil. The party was pro-slavery and was the chief cause of the Civil War. The southern Democrats fought for slavery while the northern Democrats opposed Abraham Lincoln at every turn, attempting to get him to let the south secede and continue slavery. The Democrats started an immoral war with Mexico, stole land from the Indians, and were the authors of genocide against peaceful Indians in the Midwest. The infamous Trail of Tears was the direct result of Andrew Jackson's Indian removal policy. For more on this see my book *Hidden History* on Amazon.[70]

The Democrats were complicit in the subjugation of minorities and weaker nations to steal land for the personal profit of the politicians who championed government policies that resulted in death and suffering for untold thousands. They opposed civil rights and have been on the

---

[68] *https://www.stonecoldtruth.com/the-numbers-dont-lie-proof-of-fake-news-confirmed/*

[69] *Ibid*

[70] *Hidden History: The Untold Story of the Democratic Party. Avaiable at this link: https://www.amzn.com/B08VRFLQ5V*

wrong side of history in nearly every major foreign or domestic policy of the United States. Long known as "the party of evil," the Democratic Party today has turned hostile to capitalism, free enterprise, individual freedom, and Christianity. It is gravitating towards hedonism, socialism, perversion, and totalitarianism.

To facilitate turning America into a one-party state and maintaining its power indefinitely, the Democratic Party has opened our southern border to the world. Over a million people a year are pouring in from countries all over the world. Anyone anywhere who wants to live in America can simply go to Mexico and then walk right over the border into America. The Border Patrol will then pick them up, provide free hotel accommodations, free medical, and food stamps. Then they will fly them to wherever they want to live in the United States. No other country in the world does something so insane. The plan is for these illegal aliens to vote Democrat in every election.

As mentioned previously, the Democrat Party used the pandemic as an excuse to issue a massive number of mail-in ballots and circumvent the strict laws surrounding their use. Those laws were set up by the state legislatures, as per the U.S. Constitution. In disregard of those laws, Democrat Secretaries of State and other officials ordered that those laws not be followed. Even though this was a clear violation of the Constitution, the Supreme Court lacked the fortitude and wisdom to deal with it. Vice President Pence also failed to demand the votes be re-certified.

As Democrat Rahm Emanuel, former White House Chief of Staff for President Barack Obama said, *"You never let a serious crisis go to waste. And what I mean by that – it's an opportunity to do things you think you could not do before."* The Democratic Party has milked the pandemic for all its worth – stealing elections, trampling on individual rights, and pushing for a socialist America – doing what they could not do before.

13

Conclusion

In this final chapter, I want to delineate actions that may be taken to protect oneself and one's family from the effects of the Covid conspiracy. Step one in that plan is to procure ivermectin. Chapter 10 has told you how to do that. Once you have that medicine on hand you no longer have to live in fear of Covid as many on the left want you to. In that regard, I want to reiterate that I only advocate consultation with a licensed medical doctor and that you follow his or her directions. That is the legal and safe way to go and it is the only way that I would recommend.

Guard Your Family

The next step is to insulate yourself as much as possible from the dangers brought upon society by liberals using the pandemic to advance their insane policies. The government is currently printing money to the tune of trillions of dollars, which is going to throw gasoline on the fires of inflation already raging. When that happens the value of the dollar is going to plummet. Proverbs 27:12 says,

The prudent sees danger and hides himself, but the simple go on and suffer for it.

In the book of Daniel, we read that God warned Daniel that a seven-year famine was coming so that he could prepare for it. Daniel ordered Egypt to store food. As a result, many lives were saved. Many Christian leaders today are giving warnings that it would be wise to have a reserve of food and basic supplies in case of a national emergency. I am not talking about panic buying. I am talking about budgeting a little extra every month to gradually build up a personal storehouse for your family.

You can order buckets of "survival food" from many places on the Internet, but that is an expensive way to go. My wife and I bought several 25-pound bags of rice, beans, and oats and it only cost a couple hundred dollars. Then I ordered Mylar bags on the Internet and some oxygen absorbers and resealed everything in the Mylar bags. Our supply will now stay fresh for decades.

Guard Your Nation

Many people think, and I used to be one of them, that if we simply have a good president, all will be well. I no longer have such illusions. President Trump was one of the best presidents America has had, yet the deep state liberals were able to unseat him. What I now realize is that we must take back America at the local level.

Every God-fearing American must become involved in local politics and in local school boards and ensure that the policies of the Democratic Party are brought to a decisive end. While our founders never believed that the state should affect Church affairs, they did profoundly advocate that the morals of the Church should positively influence the state.

Election reform is essential. We need voter ID laws in all the states, and mail-in voting must be kept to a minimum. The electronic voting machines have to go. These matters are under the control of the legislatures of each state. Everyone needs to write to their representatives and push for election reform as soon as possible. It must be done before the next election. For more information and to find out how you can help, go to FrankSpeech.com

Last, but certainly not least, is this: America has a spiritual problem. As a nation, we have turned away from

God and kicked His moral principles to the curb. We have turned toward unrighteousness and debauchery. Many Christians are afraid to espouse God's laws on sexual sin because of a fear of being called a homophobe. Even our leaders promote wickedness and call evil good and good evil. Over two centuries ago, President George Washington in his inaugural address uttered these prophetic words:

The propitious smiles of heaven can never be expected on a nation that disregards the eternal rules of order and right, which heaven itself has ordained.

This is profound wisdom that we ignore at our peril. If America is to enjoy the blessings of God there must be a spiritual awakening. If that does not happen, dark and terrible times are ahead. America is on the brink. Actually, it is beyond that. The dark and terrible times are upon us and America has gone over the precipice. Yet there is hope if America can be turned back to God.

We must also take back our schools, many of which have been co-opted by liberals who indoctrinate students with the destructive beliefs of the left. Many public schools teach that Marxism, socialism, transgenderism, Islam, global warming, abortion, premarital sex, and homosexuality are all acceptable philosophies, practices, and lifestyles. These are all positions championed by the Democratic Party.

A child's indoctrination begins in grade school and continues through college. Statistics show that a child in public school is much more likely to grow up and vote Democrat than one in a charter or private school. This is why Democrats oppose charter schools. For every child that escapes the indoctrination of the public school system, there is one less mind for them to corrupt. We must push for school choice in every state. President Ronald Reagan warned,

Freedom is never more than one generation away from extinction. We didn't pass it to our children in the bloodstream. It must be fought for, protected, and handed on for them to do the same, or one day we will spend our sunset years telling our children and our children's children what it was once like in the United States where men were free.

In many of our nation's churches, where once the pulpits were aflame with passion for fairness, justice, and righteousness, there is now a growing apathy, fed by an underlying philosophy that Christianity and politics should never be mixed. Too many preachers no longer preach against governmental foolishness and injustice and instead confine themselves to religious matters within their own Christian bubble. This is a great danger and is not how it used to be. In my book *Hidden History,* I speak at length about the moral responsibility Christians have to be involved in civic duty to our government.

Before and during the American revolution, pastors taught and spoke from the pulpit on political topics and issues. In her book, The New England Clergy and the American Revolution, Alice Baldwin demonstrates that the political activism of Christian pastors and their bold rhetoric from the pulpit is what formed the consensus of American sentiment on freedom and justice and that without their political vocalizations to their congregations, there would have been no American revolution. Her book contains many examples of fiery sermons that touched upon the politics of the time.

If it were not for a great Christian revival that swept the nation in the early 19th century, the slaves would not have been set free when they were. The Second Great Awakening was a Protestant revival that began around 1790 and continued into the 1830s. Historians believe that ideas put forth during this revival inspired abolitionists to oppose slavery.

Before and during the Civil War, it was from the pulpits, which were anything but silent, that the impetus to free the slaves was heard. Not only was slavery denounced by northern pastors, but preachers openly criticized pro-slavery politicians right from the pulpit. One must ask, how much longer would slavery have continued if preachers of the time had been silent on political matters?

The time has come when our pulpits must once again flame with righteousness and indignation over the flaunting of God's laws and the utter disregard for decency and the abandonment of all common sense. As our Lord chased the money changes from the temple, so must the moral majority of America use the ballot box to chase the depraved from the halls of Congress.

Jesus and his love, his forgiveness, his righteousness, his teaching about the judgment to come – all these truths and more must be proclaimed in every venue, in the backyards, the streets, the alleys, in the marketplace, in homes, and in Congress. The message of Christ must go forth from the Christian pulpit and permeate the podiums of political discourse where it can change the course of a wayward nation before it is too late.

Guard Yourself

There is one last thing that one must do to be prepared for the future. It is not really the last thing but should be the first thing in order of priority. And that is to make Jesus Christ the center of your life. Let me tell you why. Jesus is coming back soon. Very soon. Be ready. Make sure your family is in church so that all of your children are ready.

The Bible describes an event that has come to be called "The Rapture." Here is what the Bible says about that great occurrence:

But let me reveal to you a wonderful secret. We will not all die, but we will all be transformed! It will happen in a moment, in the blink of an eye, when the last trumpet is blown. For when the trumpet sounds, those who have died will be raised to live forever. And we who are living will also be transformed. For our dying bodies must be transformed into bodies that will never die; our mortal bodies must be transformed into immortal bodies. (1 Corinthians 15:51-53)

We tell you this directly from the Lord: We who are still living when the Lord returns will not meet him ahead of those who have died. For the Lord himself will come down from heaven with a commanding shout, with the voice of the archangel, and with the trumpet call of God. First, the believers who have died will rise from their graves. Then, together with them, we who are still alive and remain on the earth will be caught up in the clouds to meet the Lord in the air. Then we will be with the Lord forever. (1 Thessalonians 4:15-17)

You also must be ready all the time, for the Son of Man will come when least expected. (Luke 12:40)

People didn't realize what was going to happen until the flood came and swept them all away. That is the way it will be when the Son of Man comes. Two men will be working together in the field; one will be taken, the other left. (Matthew 24:39-40)

When people are saying, "Everything is peaceful and secure," then disaster will fall on them as suddenly as a pregnant woman's labor pains begin. And there will be no escape. (1 Thessalonians 5:3)

This is going to happen. Some people laugh at the idea. The Bible predicted they would:

Most importantly, I want to remind you that in the last days scoffers will come, mocking the truth and following their own desires. They will say, "What happened to the promise that Jesus is coming again? (2 Peter 3:3-4)

Scripture tells us that the end-time prophesies will be fulfilled and that even though it may be a while, it will one day certainly come:

For the revelation awaits an appointed time; it speaks of the end and will not prove false. Though it linger, wait for it; it will certainly come and will not delay. (Habakkuk 2:3)

At some point, and I think it will be soon, Jesus will come back and take all the Christians to heaven. Only those who have made Jesus their Lord and put their faith in Him will be making that trip. All others will be left behind. The Bible says that once the Church is out of the way, there will be nothing left to hold back the forces of evil. Those who have wanted licentious lawlessness and lude sensuality will finally control the world. They will get a leader that champions their wickedness – the Antichrist. If you want to read about the horrors that happen then, read Revelation, the last book of the Bible. It tells of the terrors of the Tribulation. Trust me, you don't want to be here for that.

If you have not repented of your sins and turned to Jesus to be saved, do it now while there is still time. You can be saved and heaven-bound right now. All it takes is a change of heart, a desire to forsake sin and do right. And then put your faith in Christ. You can do it right now. A simple prayer to God is where it all begins. Invite Christ into your heart and He will change you from the inside out into a new person. He won't change you into someone you won't like or recognize. He will make you the best you that you can be, and you will love it! The Bible says:

If you confess with your mouth that Jesus is Lord and believe in your heart that God raised him from the dead, you will be saved. For with the heart one believes and is justified, and with the mouth one confesses and is saved. For the Scripture says, 'Everyone who believes in him will not be put to shame.' (Romans 10:9-11)

Once you have done that take your first step of obedience and get baptized into the Christian faith and become part of a Bible-preaching church. If you already know the Lord, then now is a time to draw near to God as never before. Staying close to Jesus will help you have the insight you need to navigate the difficult times we are in. God will give you direction, perhaps through dreams or intuition, to know what to do to keep your family safe.

The Covid conspiracy is real and dangerous, but God has His agenda too. On His side are the armies of heaven and myriads of angels. Scripture tells us, *"When the enemy shall come in like a flood, the Spirit of the Lord shall lift up a standard against him."* (Isaiah 59:19) God is doing that now. The word tells us: *"Be on the alert, stand firm in the faith, act like men, be strong."* (1 Corinthians 16:13) May the Church stand ready to obey His every command and provide solace amid the storm. God has a plan for every nation and every individual, a plan that includes salvation and protection for you and your family and hopefully, with work and prayer, redemption for our wayward nation.

* * *

Reviews help others decide if a book has information that they would be interested in. If you care to leave a review it will be appreciated! You may use the link below to leave a review:

www.GreatRead.us/rend

To see other books by this author visit –

www.GreatRead.us/books

These titles are available from the same author...

Learn fascinating and comforting truths, such as...

- ➢ Why Christians don't need to fear the future.
- ➢ Scriptural proof of a pre-tribulation Rapture.
- ➢ Recent signs that we are in the last days.
- ➢ The mystery of the 7th Kingdom prophecy.
- ➢ The identity of Babylon the Great.
- ➢ Principals for interpreting prophecy.
- ➢ How to be saved.

With careful historical analysis and fresh insight, the author explains biblical prophecy in plain language.

Available at: https://www.GreatRead.us/end2

True Stories of Real Miracles. Read about…

> ➢ Spiritual Gifts of Power.
> ➢ Lives Saved by Angelic Intervention.
> ➢ Deliverance from Demonic Possession.
> ➢ The Miracle of Salvation in Jesus.
> ➢ Twelve Heartwarming Miraculous Short Stories.

This book is a page-turner that is guaranteed to help you expect God to work miracles in your life and to trust him through times when he doesn't.

Available at: https://www.amzn.com/B087RC7L5N

What happens to a Christian when they die? Does one go immediately to be with the Lord or is one unconscious until the resurrection?

This book thoroughly examines the issue. The author makes an airtight case from scripture and from the writings of early Christendom that is irrefutable; the Bible and historic Christianity both deny the doctrine of soul sleep and affirm the immortality of the soul.

Available at: https://www.amzn.com/B089M6P615